# *Relationshift*

*Therefore if you have any encouragement*
*from being united with Christ,*
*if any comfort from his love,*
*if any common sharing in the Spirit,*
*if any tenderness and compassion,*
*then make my joy complete by*
*being like-minded, having the same love,*
*being one in spirit and of one mind.*

Philipians 2:1-2

# Relationshift

Changing the Conversation
about
Men and Women in the Church

A. Sue Russell

Jackie Roese

CROSS

PERSPECTIVES

Whittier, California

*Cross Perspectives*
*Whittier, California*
*crossperspectives@gmail.com*

Greek Empire, Figure 1 by Russell from Diadochi PT.svg: Luigi Chiesa (talk · contribs) derivative work: Morningstar1814 [CC BY-SA 4.0 (https://creativecommons.org/licenses/by-sa/4.0)], via Wikimedia Commons.

*Cover and graphics by David Russell*

*Printed in the United States of America*

*1081518*

Names: Russell, A. Sue | Jackie Roese

Title: Relationshift Changing the Conversation about Men and Women in the Church, / A. Sue Russell; Jackie Roese.

Description: Whittier, California : Cross Perspectives, 2018 | Discussion of new ways of looking at the relationships between men and women in the church and in the home.

Identifiers: ISBN 978-1-64047-004-0 (soft-cover) | ISBN 978-1-64047-006-4 (epub)

Library of Congress Control Number: 2018909009
CrossPerspectives, Whittier, CA

## Dedication

We dedicate this book to the men in our lives
who have mentored, empowered and showed us
what it means to live as brothers and sisters in Christ.

These powerful advocates are worthy of special
mention: Dr. Haddon Robison, Ray Befus,
Ben Pinto, Jimmy Libau,
Dr. Sherwood Lingenfelter, and
Dr. S. Scott Bartchy.

Most of all we dedicate this book to our husbands
who believe in us, love us,
and walk with us as partners and friends.
You are great men of the faith!
David Russell
Steve Roese

# Table of Contents

1   A New Conversation . . . . . . . . . . . . . . 1

2   Partners in Paradise . . . . . . . . . . . . . . 19

3   Relationships in Ruin . . . . . . . . . . . . . 35

4   Relationships Renewed . . . . . . . . . . . 57

5   The Promise Becomes a Reality . . . . 75

6   Siblings in Christ . . . . . . . . . . . . . . . . 97

7   Siblings in the World . . . . . . . . . . . . 109

8   The Prickly Passage . . . . . . . . . . . . . 121

9   Conclusion . . . . . . . . . . . . . . . . . . . . 141

    Acknowledgments . . . . . . . . . . . . . . . 153

    End Notes . . . . . . . . . . . . . . . . . . . . . 157

    Biographies of the Authors . . . . . . . . . . . 180

*Chapter 1*

# A New Conversation

Another book about gender roles in the church? Aren't there enough books out there on this subject? Is there any point to further debate? The debate about the roles of men and women is argued primarily from two positions, each well-defined and well-defended. The same contested passages are cited on both sides of the debate to support either: 1) an egalitarian position that argues the Bible does not support distinct gender roles or hierarchy between these roles or 2) a complementarian position that argues there is a biblical normative order between men and women in the home and church ministry, and this order includes specific gender-based roles and a hierarchy for these roles.[1] Both sides of the debate affirm the equal value of men and women but disagree on the roles that the New Testament assigns.

I (Sue), as a New Testament scholar and trained anthropologist, have studied and lived in different cultures for over 30 years. I find that there are cultural assumptions both sides bring to the interpretation of Scripture. Let me explain. In anthropology we talk about how culture gives us particular perspectives or lenses through which we see the world. Think about sunglasses, reading glasses, or even 3D glasses and how they change how we see the world. I remember the first time I tried on polarized lenses. Wow, I was able to clearly see objects on the ocean's surface that the sun's glare had hidden, but those same lenses obscured the features on my phone. The objects had not changed, but the lenses either enhanced or obscured what I saw. Sometimes we need to put on or take off different lenses to see things from a different perspective.

The lenses we wear affect the questions we ask and, therefore, the answers we find in Scripture. In the debate about the roles of men and women, the question that has been asked is, "What does Scripture say about the roles of men and women in the home and church?" Some conclude that there are roles based on gender; others come to the conclusion that roles are based on spiritual gifting. However, both sides of the debate are looking through the same lenses—"roles."

*Relationshift: changing the conversation from roles to relationship.*

We would like to introduce a new conversation, using a different lens. Rather than asking what Scripture says about roles, we ask, "What does Scripture say about the 'relationships' between men and women?" Our conversation is about relationships, not roles. In this book we present a case that the narrative focus of the New Testament is about relationships—specifically how followers of Christ can live a new way in relationship with one another within the social roles of any society.

Every book has a story behind its creation, a reason why it was written. There are encounters, experiences, and conversations that shape the perspective of the authors and lead them to question the status quo, to dig deeply into Scripture, to critically evaluate what others have said, and sometimes to discover a different way of seeing. To really understand a book, it helps to understand the stories behind it. Both of us, Sue and Jackie, have stories that have shaped and influenced this new conversation we are sharing with you.

## Sue's Story: Missionary and Professor

Growing up, I don't ever remember being told in words or actions that there were things I should or should not enjoy as a girl. I preferred playing with G.I. Joe rather than Barbie, playing army rather than playing house. I loved baseball and played regularly in our neighborhood games. We didn't have girls my age in the neighborhood, so my best friends were boys, and they never made me feel like I didn't belong.

In school, I often played with the boys rather than the girls. I discovered boys included you if you had the skills to perform. In high school, my friends were those who excelled in sports and academics. We didn't think of ourselves in terms of gender; there were as many girls as boys included in our geeky group. Inclusion was based on what you *did* rather than who you *were*, and it was both a racially-diverse and gender-diverse group of friends. Title IX was passed while I was in high school, and because of it the coach of the boys' junior varsity baseball team allowed me to join. At first there was hesitation on the part of the boys, but soon they begrudgingly acknowledged that I was pretty good "for a girl." But the coaching I received, the hard work, and the competition left me with a love for sports and the skills to excel in college.

I was a bit different than my high school friends; they wanted to be doctors and lawyers. I, however, loved being outdoors and wanted a career that would allow me to do so. Not sure what I wanted to do,

I applied late to college and was only able to get into Humboldt State University in Northern California as a chemistry major. I discovered that I loved chemistry. My professor took note of my gifting after I received a perfect score on my sixth lab quiz in a row. (I had never heard that girls were not expected to do well in chemistry.) However, my love for being outdoors led me to change my major to forest management. In this major the labs were walks in the forest, and classes and quizzes were often conducted outside. I thoroughly enjoyed the classes and comradery. Often I was the only woman in a class of 50 men, but I discovered men would open the door for me as long as I was carrying the equipment. If there was discrimination being a woman in a traditional man's field, I never experienced it from my classmates. As long as I carried my load and did my share of the work, I was accepted.

The first place I experienced a strong voice on the capabilities of being a women was my summer job with a forest firefighting crew. Women had just been allowed to join firefighting crews, and one of the older men felt strongly that women should not be allowed to participate in fighting large project fires. These were fires over 1,000 acres and often required multiple, 20+ hour days on the fire line. The man held this view until he worked alongside two of us women on a large project fire.

Our crew of 20 was called to an area in Oregon where it was unclear if there was one fire or a thousand. While we put out numerous small fires throughout the day, we watched the smoke across the ridge grow. We knew by the size of the smoke that one fire had gotten away, and we were now facing several days on the line as the wind and heat created conditions for a quickly spreading fire. For the next 10 days we battled the fire. When the guys carried 80 pounds of water up the hill, I carried 80 pounds of water up the hill. Some days lasted 20-22 hours.

Some days we ran from flames, but as we worked on the line, keeping up with the guys on the crew, the men grew to respect the women on the crew. Even the older crew member acknowledged that women could handle the work and endurance required on a project fire. We were accepted as full members of the crew.

During my fourth year of college, I had an encounter with Christ's love, and it changed my life and my career path. I now had new goals, new desires. Two years later in 1982, I applied and was accepted with Wycliffe Bible Translators. After I finished my training, I was assigned to a language group in Southeast Asia where I began working with a group of pastors to translate the Bible into their own language. Since I was young and single, like the other young, single people in this church community, I was expected to contribute my gifts, talents, and resources to the good of the group under the leadership of the elders. There was never a distinction about whether a job best fit a man or a woman. They allocated tasks to people based on whether the person was: a) gifted by God to do the job and b) called of God to do the job. Age and gender did not have any part in the discussion. Because young women in that culture often had fewer obligations to their mothers and fathers, they were able to go to Bible college, and many became teachers in the church. Whether man or woman, those with a Bible college education were expected to use their gifts to serve the good of the church community under the leadership of the church elders. Gifts and talents did not belong to individuals but rather the group as a whole. I discovered this personally when I returned to the village after earning my first doctorate. At our first meeting the members of the translation committee discussed how they were going to use "OUR" doctorate.

The first time I encountered the debate about the role of women in the home and the church was in 2000 when I began teaching at an evangelical college in the United States. I had never been confronted with this debate before, so I began my journey into the literature. I was heartbroken at what I read and the spitefulness in which the cases on both sides of the so-called gender debate were expressed. In one book the author argued that if we were on the other side of the debate, we no longer believed in the authority of Scripture. As an anthropologist, I was also disturbed by some of the clearly, to me at least, cultural perspectives that were being expressed as biblical. Often, perhaps without realizing it, an author would start with a clear biblical statement but then place a very cultural meaning on it. As I began my theological studies, I learned more about this debate and became more uncomfortable with both sides of the argument. I found that both were based on very Western, particularly North American, biases and assumptions. Often interpretations of key passages were already decided long before exegesis was started. I realized that neither of the teachings, egalitarian or complementarian, could be applied to my church in Southeast Asia. The teachings of both sides of the debate would require an adoption of a foreign church structure that would be harmful to the life of my Southeast Asian church.

It wasn't until 2005 that I directly felt the effects of the debate in my own life in the church. Growing up I discovered I had a gift for teaching and I enjoyed it. In high school and college I had opportunities to teach mountaineering, first aid, rock climbing, etc. As a new Christian this gift was affirmed by leaders, and I was given opportunities to lead mixed gender Bible studies at college. It came easily, and I had affirmation that I was a good communicator. While overseas I was also able to teach translation principle courses, Bible studies, anthropology, and literacy classes to pastors and elders across multiple languages and ethnicities. However, in my own church in Southern

California, I discovered that although I was a gifted teacher and was teaching a university Bible class to undergraduate students, I was not allowed to teach in our mixed gender adult fellowship class because I was a woman. I found myself in a church where my spiritual gifts and academic training (by that time I had an MDiv and ThM in New Testament) could not be used.

Perhaps most disheartening was when one of the leaders explained why they didn't allow women to teach the class. His main point: "The Bible says women can't teach because they are more easily deceived." I was no longer Sue, but I was part of a class of people, i.e. "women who are more easily deceived." I felt like raising my hand and exclaiming, "Hey, I am right here! You are talking about me! Am I more easily deceived than someone without seminary training?" I was excluded not because of who I was as a person but because I belonged to the category "women." It is easier to exclude people based on their category than to exclude individuals we know. People often asked me why I stayed in the class. My reply was, "I stayed because my very presence raised the question of why a well-qualified, gifted teacher was not allowed to teach simply because she is a woman."

*It is easier to exclude people based on their category than to exclude individuals we know.*

In 1998 I married my husband David, and because of his encouragement, I decided to complete my doctoral training in New Testament studies. I looked for a program where I could combine my anthropology and biblical studies. I didn't intentionally set out to study or write about the gender debate or about roles of men and women in the church. Others had far more expertise in classical texts than I

7

could ever master in my lifetime. But as I began to use concepts from anthropology to explore the writings of the New Testament, I discovered a consistent way of reading Scriptures about social relationships that gave a new perspective on the seemingly contradictory statements about men and women. It also provided consistent interpretation of passages on race, ethnicity, class, and other social categories that divide us. As a former missionary, I was excited because this way of looking at Scripture provided principles that could be applied cross-culturally in ways that reflect the central themes about social relationships in the Kingdom of God but still allow different communities to determine what that looks like in their own cultures. I discovered that the Scripture does not eradicate our social categories but rather discusses a new way of relating within our cultural social statuses and roles. My study concluded that the focus of New Testament passages about social relationships does not reinforce roles and statuses but rather describes how we can live out a new kind of relationship, as brothers and sisters, within roles and statuses of our culture.

*Scripture does not eradicate our social categories but rather discusses a new way of relating within our cultural social statuses and roles.*

As I began a conversation with others, I found that many others were also looking for a new way to talk about gender and gender roles in the church. Then Jackie found me, and we started a conversation that led to the writing of this book. While my encounter with the gender debate has been primarily in academia, Jackie has lived this debate as a woman who is a leader in the church.

## *Jackie's Story: Preacher and Pastor*

I grew up in a farm family in upstate New York. God was a non-entity in our home, at my school, and in my friendships. I don't recall knowing any Christians, and I never read a Bible nor went to church. It was in college where I was introduced to Jesus. It was a short few months from that introduction that I would come to faith and then marry my husband Steve. The pastor who officiated our wedding had attended Dallas Theological Seminary (DTS). When we decided to get serious about Jesus, we thought we, too, should go to school to get to know Jesus better. Being that DTS was "the" seminary (or so I thought, not realizing there were other options), we moved to Dallas, Texas.

Alas, I ended up as a brand-new Christian sitting around a table with students, spouses, and a host professor, eating Texas BBQ at our seminary orientation. As we chatted, I talked with the other women. One woman had five kids and mentioned that one of her son's names was Micah. "Micah. What a cool name," I thought. So I said, "I've never heard that name before. Where did you get that?" Everyone at the table turned to look at me, including our host professor, Dr. Eugene Merrell, a world-renowned Old Testament professor. I knew I had committed a faux pas, but I couldn't imagine what it was. The point is that I was as green as they come. I had arrived at seminary without any Bible knowledge. I didn't know the story of Jonah or Abraham or the books of the Bible or that my first encounter of eye-rolling, head-tilted, confused look of "huh?" from conservative Christians would not be my last.

It took almost eight years to graduate, mostly because I kept having kids, and mothering was a priority. I arrived in Dallas with Hunter, our one-year-old, and pregnant with my second. Hunter was 20 months old when his brother, Hampton, was born. Nineteen months later, I gave birth to our third child, Madison.

At 28, I had three children under the age of three-and-a-half. I went slowly, one class per semester until Madison went to kindergarten. The pace worked for me. I had lots to learn and was still trying to figure out how Jesus walked on water. So I completed all the extra reading assignments and chased rabbits down trails. I loved the stimulation at a time when my only social life was with toddlers. Besides, what was the hurry? I had no plans to go into ministry. I just wanted to get to know Jesus better.

Because I was on lock-down in that tiny apartment caring for those small children, I spent little time on campus or in the church world. This meant I wasn't exposed to many other Christians or Christian thinking. I missed out on the theological debates on campus, including the debate on the role of women. In fact, years would pass in my education before I even knew there was a "women's issue." It would be a few years later when the women's issue would cause the Christian community to do a huge, head-tilted-in-confusion "huh."

Over time during those years in that apartment, I came to know Jesus as the lover of my soul, and I also learned how he had gifted me. I served in Vacation Bible School (VBS) and eventually had a group of women in my home for Bible study. It became evident I was gifted by the Spirit to herald the Scriptures. It would take three years after that home Bible study for our women's pastor to invite me to teach at the women's Bible study in our church. In my mind I said "no," but "yes" came out of my mouth. I spent the next six years volunteering as a Bible teacher and author of Bible study materials.

When I came on staff at a church, I inherited a well-established women's Bible study. At one time we had seven teachers on the teaching team. We were writing and publishing curriculum, and we had over 60 table leaders and 900 women attending. There was a buzz among our women, and they shared their excitement with their husbands. Women started asking if their husbands could attend the study, too. I wasn't keen on the idea. In the conservative evangelical world, women are less apt to speak up about the Bible and theology when men are present. I longed for women to be empowered by hearing themselves talk about Jesus and Scripture.

But I knew trouble was brewing when men started harassing our men's pastor: "Why isn't our study as good as the women's?" Nothing good comes out of questions like that. I knew men don't like to be one-upped by women, so I scheduled a dinner to discuss the issue. My colleague was "man enough" to admit the comparison had been difficult for him. I felt anger that my brother in Christ

*Ministry is not a competition; it's collaboration.*

had been belittled like a kid being teased on the playground. It shouldn't be this way. I shouldn't have to be less so he could feel like more, nor should he feel less because a woman was succeeding. Ministry is not a competition; it's collaboration. Yet in order for us to collaborate, my brothers needed to be assured I was not a threat to their masculinity.

Perhaps the most public experience of how the gender debate affects the church is when gifted women are not allowed to use their gifts for the benefit of the church. Over the years it became clear I was not only gifted to preach, but I had been called and I was good at it. (In Romans 12 Paul tells us to have an accurate view of ourselves, not too high or too low.) After a year-and-a-half study, our elders decided that women could preach from the pulpit. In fact, I would be the first woman to preach since the inception of that church. Plenty of people were not happy. It was a hot Texas morning in August of 2008. Sunday attendance was usually down in August, but not this day. On this day the sanctuary was filled to the brim, all 2,250 seats. The air was filled with tension and anticipation. Channel 8's camera crew lined the back wall waiting to capture the "event" for the evening news. I sat in the front row, center left from the stage. Directly behind me were my husband, three kids, and a few close friends. My heart felt like it was beating outside my chest. It was a good thing I had a jacket on to hide the underarm perspiration. Don't get me wrong: I was not afraid of preaching. I had preached hundreds of messages, but not to this crowd and not under these circumstances. Pastor Andy McQuitty sat to my left, and my bodyguard, Bryan, sat to my right. At a solid 5-foot-2, I tend to feel overpowered when standing next to men of Bryan's stature of 6-foot-5 and 230 pounds, but on this day I was comforted.

Dressed in black with a slicked-back ponytail, arms crossed like a CIA agent, Bryan communicated to all present, "Don't even think of trying to accost her." There had been a lot of adversity building up to this day. *The Dallas Morning News* ran an article with my picture, "Woman's turn in the pulpit...generates buzz, beefs." A sister church alerted other conservative evangelical pastors of the "grave moral concern" at Irving Bible Church (IBC). Mark Bailey, president of Dallas Theological Seminary, left our congregation, and his departure caused a stir at the seminary as well as churches pastored by former seminary students. The blogosphere went wild with affirmation and assailants alike. In light of this, our leadership decided Bryan should serve as my bodyguard for all three services. As the initial service began, my heart beat faster and faster. Jason, our worship pastor, took us to the throne through song. With all the chaos ensuing, I was never more grateful for song to center my mind and heart on Jesus. Just as Jason finished the last set of songs, Pastor Andy walked up on stage and approached the podium. He welcomed everyone and then proceeded to share how the elders of IBC (all men), after a year-and-a-half study, concluded women could preach from the pulpit. Then he asked the audience to welcome the first woman to preach in our church's 40-year history. I took a deep breath and walked up on stage.

In seminary I also experienced another narrative about the relationship between men and women that is common in our churches, a "romantic-danger" narrative. In my first-year doctoral course, the classroom was set up with four tables arranged in a square formation. The professor was seated at the front of the class. As I stood in the doorway, I scanned the room for Maxie, the only other woman on the student roster. "Where is she? She must be late." I hoped to sit next to her. Instead a middle-aged man waved for me to sit next to him. I was relieved he took the initiative. The rest of the class just stared, not knowing what to do with my presence. I thought to myself, "When is Maxie coming?" Our professor went around the tables, asking each of us to share something about ourselves. That's when I learned Maxie was a male pastor from Jamaica. Talk about disappointed. I would be the only female in a class of 27 students, all male pastors and me. The men in my class—and let me say they were wonderful, godly men— didn't have a clue what to do with me, a female-embodied spirit.

For two weeks the guys headed out to lunch while I stayed behind eating alone in the lunchroom. I know they felt bad, but they had the romantic-danger narrative running through their heads. You don't take a woman to lunch. You don't get in a car alone with a woman. You don't have a woman in your office with the door closed. I felt cheated because I knew I was missing out on great conversations about homiletics, the church, the Kingdom, and the like that continued from the classroom. I longed to benefit, grow, and be transformed and to have iron sharpen iron (Proverbs 27:17), but my femaleness apparently screamed, "Danger! Danger!" to them, so I was left out.

Housing for my second-year residency was a continued reminder that being female was "a problem." As the only woman, I was housed in a separate place from the men. I stayed in a big, old, musty-smelling inn with dark hallways, just outside of the Boston city limits—alone, all by myself. The male students stayed together in the yellow house adjacent to the inn. To attend class, we drove 15 minutes to an area of Boston deemed not all that safe. At least, that was the warning given by the seminary, and it turned out to be warranted since a man was murdered outside our building during our residency there. The night I arrived at the inn, I made up my mind to catch a ride with one of the guys at least for the first day or until I felt secure driving by myself. The next morning I walked into the breakfast area where all the guys were eating. I noticed Bill, one of my cohorts, sitting a few tables back to my right. My built-up fear of feeling unsafe at the seminary burst while I stood at the entrance of the room. "Bill," I blurted out for all to hear, "can you give me a ride to class?"

*...my femaleness apparently screamed, "Danger! Danger!" to them, so I was left out.*

Everyone froze, mid-motion, spoons and coffee cups suspended in midair. I stood there thinking, "Oh brother, you've got to be kidding me?" Once again I faced down that romantic-danger narrative. Their fear of me and my womanhood overshadowed my legitimate fear for my safety. Good Christian men would rather "protect" themselves (and their fear of lust) than protect a neighbor. I had had it. I wasn't going to let it dominate the landscape anymore. I wanted more for me—and them. So I did what I learned to do growing up: I called it out. Isn't that what we teach—that communication is key to relationships? I decided it was time to communicate a new narrative. I hoped my narrative would put them at ease, and we could get to learning homiletics together. So standing there, overlooking the room, I said, "I don't want to have sex with you. I just want a ride. As your sister in Christ, I want a ride because I'm afraid. I don't want to get raped." There was this nervous chuckle, but also an awkward relief because we had gotten it out in the open. We finished eating breakfast, and I caught a ride to class with Bill.

Now I know what some are thinking: "But, Jackie, aren't we playing with fire by insisting on a different narrative?" No, in fact I think the brother-sister narrative is a biblical narrative that has gotten lost and is long overdue in our oversexed culture. Take into account that the brother-sister relationship is the one that is carried into the new heavens and new earth. The brother-sisterhood narrative forces us to reckon that the Garden story is about more than marriage; it's about

> *The brother-sister narrative, is a biblical narrative that has gotten lost and is long overdue in our oversexed culture.*

man and woman in community, male and female acting as a royal priesthood, ruling and subduing the whole earth on God's behalf—together!

## Conclusion

We have told our stories because they are like many of the stories that we regularly hear. Perhaps you are thinking of your own experiences as we have talked about ours. Perhaps, like us, you are confused because you don't fit the gender expectations that you have been taught in your church. Perhaps you are one of the women or men who has gifts that don't fit the roles you are "supposed" to fulfill. You may want to "check out" of the church because you've heard that if you don't agree or believe a certain way, you must not believe in the Bible. Sadly, perhaps you have experienced abuse and exclusion because of some church's teachings. Or maybe you have been hurt and are ready to leave the church because you do not feel valued or cannot use your gifts. Or you feel pressured into positions that don't fit your gifting. Or you feel like you have been villainized for just being who you are. We can resonate. You are not alone. Don't lose heart, because we think there is a far more universal narrative in Scripture about men and women than a discussion of roles and rules.

Perhaps you also have found the writings on the roles of men and women in the church do not resonate with you. You have critically analyzed them and have found they are lacking, or you can't take one side or the other because there is truth in both. You want to be faithful to Scripture, but both sides seem to be emphasizing select portions of Scripture to make their case. They did not resonate with me (Sue) because I saw that both positions came from cultural assumptions and could not be applied cross-culturally. Or perhaps some of you don't like the caricature of the debate and the divisiveness it causes among family and friends. Or perhaps you are new to the faith and are just learning about different perspectives and love the respected leaders on both sides so don't know what to believe or what it means for you and your church; you feel like you have to choose sides and there is no good side to choose. Please know that you are not alone.

The purpose of this book is to open a different conversation about men and women working together. It takes a different approach to Scripture by looking through new lenses—that of relationships. Rather than looking at specific verses or the meaning of particular words, we will take a broader look at what Jesus and Paul understood to be a new way of relating in the Kingdom of God. This new way of relating is not just about the relationship between men and women, but it is about relating across ethnicity, class, age, and whatever other boundaries separate us from one another and lead to division, exclusion, and dominance. This book is about a new way of living and loving others in a way that we were meant to live from the beginning—as brothers and sisters in Christ. It is about restoring the partnership, the love, the unity that we were created to have with one another. To fully understand the way we were meant to be, we need to start at the beginning when man and woman were created for and lived in partnership with God, with each other, and with creation.

*Chapter 2*

# Partners in Paradise

My (Jackie) friend Carrie burst into Gloria Estefan's song "Turn the Beat Around" with as much vigor and passion as Gloria herself.

> *"Turn the beat around*
> *Love to hear the passion*
> *Turn it upside down*
> *Love to hear the passion"*

Carrie belted those words with certainty for years until she discovered the lyrics actually go like this, "Turn the beat around, love to hear percussion."

Most of us pre-Googlites, those without the ability to Google, sang songs with certainty only to have it turn out that we were totally wrong and deluded. I think we do the same when it comes to Scripture. We bellow with conviction, only to discover years later that our thinking was a tad off or just plain wrong. This was true for me (Jackie) regarding my understanding of Genesis 1 and 2. I had been taught and bought the original soundtrack that sounded like, "God created man and gave him dominion over creation. Then he created Eve to help Adam with his task." The teaching emphasized the different roles—Adam was to lead, and woman follows and helps." These were the lyrics I learned in seminary; it's the song I sang. Other texts, particularly Paul's writings on women, were absorbed through presumptions of that original soundtrack until I learned my lyrics were a bit off.

When we start with presuppositions and go looking for evidence in Scripture, we tend to find it. But what happens if we change the lens and we view the Creation story through the lens of relationships? Instead of asking about roles the first man and woman had, we ask instead what kind of relationship did God intend for men and women to have with Him, with each other, and with creation. This new lens compelled us to rethink the lyrics of our Creation story. Follow along as we learn an updated version to the old soundtrack.

> *...what if we change the lens and we view the Creation story through the lens of relationships?*

"In the beginning God…" (Genesis 1:1) Let's stop here because from the get-go we need to see God as the origin, the center of our Creation story. It begins with Him—not us. Out of Him flows every good thing. God spoke and it was good.[2] All of creation flourished— the sky, sun, sea, moon…all of it! Dorothy Sayers, a contemporary of C. S. Lewis, said we are known by our work.[3] God's work in creation teaches us God is, among so many other things, all powerful, wildly generous, surpassingly good, astonishingly artistic, remarkably wise, absolute beauty, tremendously diverse, and immensely just. Psalm 119:142 states that God's justice is eternal, meaning it was present at Creation. We tend to think of justice as punishing wrongdoing or caring for those who've been wronged. But justice can also be viewed as righteousness, which is a social word; it's where relationships are right, where one uses their power, position, and resources for the advantage of others. God's justice in Creation was for us, you and me, to flourish. That's crucial to know. It informs how we are to relate to him, each other, ourselves, and the world we live in.

Have you ever noticed we tend to read Genesis 1:1-25 with a cadence? "Then God said…and it was good," "Then God said…and it was good." In many ways we've become so familiar with the words that we miss what's happening in those first 25 verses. When Moses, who is credited with recording Genesis, spoke those verses he was heralding God's direct assault on the ancient Mesopotamian gods. The Canaanites believed in over 400 gods—the sky god, sun god, moon god, etc. One by one, God refuted the Canaanite gods' legitimacy. Can you picture it? In the wilderness, before a million plus Israelites who were about to take the land of Canaan, Moses heralded God's supremacy in Genesis 1:1-25. "Sun? Nope, not a god. I made it. I'm the one and only! Moon? Nope, not a god. I made it. I'm the one and only!" Sometime later Moses continued with Exodus, "I am the LORD your God, who rescued you from the land of Egypt, the place of your slavery. You must not have any other god but me." (Exodus 20:3-4)

Ever consider why God insisted we worship no other god? I used to wonder if God was just some kind of egomaniac, but I've come to see the tender care of God in his jealousy for us. God knew we become like who or what we worship. He also knew worshiping another would destroy us, put us in bondage, and birth injustice and cruelty. Theologian Christopher Wright explains, "The tragedy of polytheism and idolatry is not the arithmetic (many gods instead of one) but that they exchange the only true source of salvation for lifeless, powerless substitutes and in doing so introduce injustice, bondage and cruelty into human life and society."[4]

Imagine with me for a moment that Irene the Israelite moves into Carla the Canaanite's neighborhood. Carla the Canaanite brings a housewarming present of unleavened bread. Carla, noticing Irene is childless, a calamity for a woman, leans in and whispers, "Our fertility goddess can help you conceive." Irene is desperate to rid herself and her family of the shame and humiliation of barrenness. Carla tempts further, "All you have to do is go to the temple and perform the behavior you wish the goddess to demonstrate. Ritual sex, that's how you can conceive!" Consider how this would introduce injustice, bondage, or cruelty into Irene's life and the life of those she loved. At one time or another, we have all leaned into those whispers and found they left us wanting.

God declares, "In the beginning God" to remind us of the one in whom to put our trust, our devotion. He's the One and Only who uses his power, position, and resources to make all of creation flourish. Then we come to the apex of God's creation in Genesis 1:26-28, "Let us make human beings in our image, to be like us." (Genesis 1:26 NLT) Man and woman are God's *imago Dei*, His image bearers.

My parents (Jackie) passed down certain characteristics and attributes to us five kids. All of us got their curly hair; the boys have more waves whereas the three girls have unruly manes. Just like our earthly parents, God our creator also passed down to his kids some of His attributes and characteristics. Some of God's attributes are incommunicable, attributes we don't share with Him. For instance, we are not all-knowing. But some of God's attributes are communicable, ones we do have, like His relationality.

God said, "Let us make mankind in our image." The word "our" (not "my") tells us something about God, doesn't it? The Father, Son, and Holy Spirit—three in one—in a conversation over us. The theological word used to describe the Trinity is perichoresis, the co-indwelling and mutual interpenetration of God's self. Theologian Alister McGrath writes that it's the idea of a "community of being" in which each person, while maintaining his/her distinctive identity, penetrates the others and is penetrated by them."[5] Our creedal statements testify that "within the Godhead there is no power struggle or hierarchy, rather there is a constancy of giving, receiving, affecting, and being affected—mutuality."[6]

"Us...Our." God is fundamentally relational, and He passed that attribute on to his kids. We were made to be in relationship with God. "Let us make mankind in our image, to be like us." He said we would be like Him, made in His likeness. We can't be like someone we don't know. To mirror people we must spend time with them, get to know their body movements, the inflection of their voice, their likes and dislikes, what causes a wince or a giggle. Intimacy was present between humans and God in the Garden. Man was with God before he was with woman (Genesis 2:15), and woman was with God before she was with man (Genesis 2:21-22). Too often I've

> *"Us...Our." God is fundamentally relational, and He passed that attribute on to his kids.*

observed women who try to make their husbands into their god, but woman's crowning relationship in Creation was with God. Perhaps it would help if we paused while reading Genesis 2:22, "Then the LORD God made a woman from the rib." (Pause here for a moment. "Who's she with? What are God and she conversing about?" Okay, now continue.) "...and he brought her to the man." "Eve was created to know and walk with God and to make him known to others by reflecting his character in her life....By naming us as his image bearers, God has made a relationship with himself the strategic center of his purpose for humanity and for the world."[7]

> "Let us make human beings in our image, to be like us..."
> So God created human beings in his own image.
> In the image of God he created them;
> male and female he created them. (Genesis 1:26-27)

In the beginning God was community, and He created us—man and woman—to be communal, to be in relationship. And like God there is no power struggle or hierarchy; rather there is a constancy of giving, receiving, affecting, and being affected—mutuality. This is the starting point of the Creation story. God put man in the Garden to tend and watch over it.[8] Then God told him he could eat from any tree but the tree of good and evil.[9] If we think about it, this is no small job. It's a huge project, and along the way there is temptation towards independence,[10] and there's one who lurks in the shadows waiting to kill and destroy (Genesis 3:1). Perhaps this is why God said next, "It is not good for the man to be alone. I will make him a suitable helper (*ezer kenegdo*) who is just right for him." (Genesis 2:18) It's the first time God said that something in Creation—aloneness—wasn't good.

*In the beginning God was community, and He created us —man and woman— to be communal, to be in relationship.*

What should we expect God to do next? Create woman, right? But he didn't. Instead He instructed man to name the animals. And what did man do? Over a span of time—it didn't happen in seconds or a day—he chose names for all the animals. He looked at the frog and said, "Hmm, I guess I'll call you frog." He looked at the dog and said, "I'll call you dog," and so on. It was through the naming process man discovered there was no other creature like him. He was alone.

Some theologians, who see through the lens of roles, view the naming of animals as an act of authority or leadership. Their logic follows that one of the ways kings in ancient Mesopotamia showed authority was by naming things. Therefore, when God had man name the animals, God was essentially identifying man as the leader in authority over everything. However, this conclusion is a misunderstanding of who the king is in the Creation story. Genesis 1 is stated much like a suzerain-vassal treaty (a treaty between two unequal parties, a powerful king and a weaker subject) of the ancient Near Eastern monarchs. God speaks. He names things. He sets His images throughout His kingdom. The king in our Creation story is not man (or woman); it is God. And even if naming the animals was some sort of act of authority, man did not name woman until after the Fall.[11] Furthermore, this passage is not about roles (leadership and authority), but rather it's about relationships—the problem of "aloneness." The solution to aloneness is "knownness," being known. Naming the animals enabled man to know who he was not, but he still didn't have a mirror to help him know who he was. We come to fully know ourselves through relationships, and we more fully reflect God when we are communal. Leadership or role isn't the beat of this song; it's relationships—knownness.

The theologian St. Augustine acknowledged it, bestselling author and sociologist Brené Brown[12] identified it, and science confirms it: We have been created with an inherent desire to belong, to know and be known. Did you know the brain, when free from cognitive tasks, defaults to social thinking? Contemplate that for a moment. Our brain's default mode is social. Did you know babies come out of the womb looking for someone who's looking for them? Their facial muscles, mouth movements, and eye contact are designed to woo someone to "find them." Neuroscience tells us our brain responds to affirmation from loved ones in the same way it responds when we eat sweets. (See, chocolate is good for you!) And when we are rejected, dumped,

*We come to fully know ourselves through relationships, and we more fully reflect God when we are communal.*

or unfriended, our brain responds the same as it responds to physical pain. In fact, some studies suggest that taking an aspirin can reduce social pain much like it reduces physical pain.[13] Science confirms what God is communicating in Genesis 1 and 2: humans were made to be social, to know and be known by others!

Back to the Genesis story. After a long while of naming animals, God put man to sleep, took a rib from him, and created woman. He brought the woman to the man, and man responded, "Bone of my bone, flesh of my flesh." (Genesis 2:23) This is not a man objectifying a woman, "Hey, she's a hot babe." Sexism did not exist in the Garden. This is the language of poetry; it's the language of wonder. It's as if man is saying, "Finally, someone who is more like me than any other creature. Finally, someone who can help me order myself."

This fits with the meaning of "suitable helper" (ezer kenegdo) in Genesis 2:20. Suitable (kenegdo) means corresponding, partner, a face-to-face relationship. Woman's presence is an invitation for man to come out of himself and into otherness, to turn away from his aloneness and independence toward face-to-face relationship and the mystery of interdependence. Here God was not defining roles but a relationship.

We associate "helper" (ezer) with images such as mommy's little helper or an assistant at work, but those images don't do justice to the Hebrew word ezer. Ezer is used 21 times in the Old Testament, twice in Genesis (2:18 & 20), three times pertaining to the nation of Israel's appeal for military assistance (Isaiah 30:5, Ezekiel 12:14 and Daniel 11:34), and 16 times for God as Israel's helper (e.g. Exodus 18:4, Deuteronomy 33:7, 26, & 29, Psalm 70:5). Of those 16 references, "helper" corresponds to words such as rescue, protection, provider, deliverer, and strength of a warrior. When was the last time you heard a preacher say that women are providers or protectors? In fact, today those terms are associated with masculinity, right? The point is that this is not a child helping mom bake cookies, nor is it a woman answering the phones for the boss. She is an ezer, a mutual partner. When we consider the massive vision God set before man and woman in Genesis 1:26-28 to care, create, and cultivate civilization in ways that allow all of creation to flourish, it was going to require a warrior like her.

> 26. Then God said, "Let us make human beings in our
> image, to be like us. They will reign over the fish in the
> sea, the birds in the sky, the livestock, all the wild animals
> on the earth, and the small animals that scurry along the
> ground."
> 27. So, God created human beings in his own image. In
> the image of God he created them; male and female he
> created them.
> 28. Then God blessed them and said, "Be fruitful and
> multiply.[14] Fill the earth and govern it. Reign over the fish
> in the sea, the birds in the sky, and all the animals that
> scurry along the ground."[15]

Again, we draw from the ancient Near Eastern culture in order to understand the context of the passage. It was common for ancient Near Eastern monarchs to view themselves as divine image bearers, appointed representatives of God on earth. The king placed images of himself on coins and statutes throughout his kingdom to remind his subjects of his sovereignty. Remember, it's God who is King. He has established his Kingdom, and He is ruler over His world and the people He created. In Genesis 1:26-28, God appointed man and woman as his representatives on earth, walking statues if you will, "intermediaries of God's power and blessing on earth."[16] It's here He gave man and woman an enormous vision to care, create, and cultivate civilization "in His likeness." In His likeness means we must envision what God is like. What does his creation reveal about who He is? Generous, artistic, just, etc. What's most impressive about God's appointment of humankind is that in ancient Mesopotamia, ordinary people like you and me were considered incidental, merely existing to meet the whimsical needs of the gods. Imagine how the Israelites must have felt when Moses declared these words in Genesis: "You are indeed imago Dei." Imagine the society God was revealing as they lived in relationship with Him and each other. The imagery wasn't lost on Moses or those million plus weary, dusty travelers in the wilderness. Let it not be lost on us either!

In Genesis 1 God created image bearers, two distinct genders, for a shared destiny in relationship. Man and woman were not given two separate vocations or roles, nor is one gender less than the other. Genesis bears witness that both genders together in relationship will rule and subdue as representatives of their King Creator.

Reign (or dominion) is a royal word meaning to govern or steward. Turning God's raw materials into a fully flourishing civilization would not be easy. Human beings would turn grapes into wine, sound into music, rocks into roads, dye into colors, and trees into homes. This was no small vision. It would take both man and woman working together: side by side, collaborating, giving, receiving, affecting, and being affected by each other – mutuality. Besides the need for one another, let's be honest, it is definitely more fun to work together than to go it alone.

This leads me to the other mandate—to subdue or enslave. This speaks of military enemies; it indicates hostility, something to be conquered. "Despite the sermons we've heard, Eden was not a safe place. There are dangerous trees and the threat of death for disobedience."[17] Danger lurked in the shadows of Genesis 2:15-17 and 3:1-5. The evil one longs to devour God's dreams for humanity. When I think of what man and woman were up against, both the magnitude of creating civilization and the weightiness of withstanding evil, they desperately needed each other. It makes me think of that team-building exercise where you sit on the floor with another person sitting with their back against yours, interlocking each other's arms. Together you push with equal strength to lift the both of you off the floor into a standing position. Man and woman using

*The vision set for man and woman is enormous.*

their mind, body, and soul to lift each other up. It's what it looks like to reflect our Creator, and it is what it takes to carry out our King Creator's mission for his Kingdom on earth. The vision set for man and woman is enormous. It's so immense we need everyone. We have to ask though, "Is it possible that the reason we sideline people due to race, gender, education, class, and religious traditions is because our vision of God's Kingdom is too small?"

My husband Steve (Jackie) is the president of Water Is Basic, an NGO (non-governmental organization) that provides clean water in South Sudan. The country, which has been at war for over 50 years, recently broke out in civil war—again. Upon the arrival of insurgents, villagers hid in the river wading amongst hippos to hide from the rebels. At nightfall when it was safe to come out, they swam their drenched bodies to shore, only to discover that nine of their children had drowned. Evil is present in South Sudan, but it's also present in my neighborhood. My friend shared that she was sexually abused as a child. One in four women in America are sexually abused, and one in three women will experience some form of domestic violence in their lifetime. Evil is present in our backyard, and I wonder if we truly comprehend the evil we are up against. If we did, we'd have everyone—wherever, whenever, however—a force of warriors fanning out in God's Kingdom. We need everyone, both men and women, in the fight to carry out God's mission.

This takes us to man and woman's relationship. We don't have volumes written on their story; we don't even have chapters. We have Genesis 2 to review. And although today Genesis 2 tends to be read as merely a relationship between husband and wife, we (as well as the early church fathers) suggest it encompasses all relationships between men and women. To put it simplistically, if Genesis 1 and 2 is only about the relationship between husband and wife, then some of humankind is excluded from the Creation story such as John the Baptist and the Apostle Paul as well as 51% of American women living without a significant man in their life. Scholar Bernd Wannenwetsch notes that St. Augustine acknowledged man and woman's relationship at Creation to be about humanity first, sexuality second. Removal of a rib indicates companionship. There was companionship between man and woman prior to procreation. There was a brother–sister relationship/

union that was established whether there was sex or not. Sex aided the union, but still there was that union.[18] This is in line with the signposts to our future in the new heaven and new earth.[19] Jesus indicated we are not married in the new heaven and new earth. Therefore, it seems the relationship that is present in eternity is familial, that of brother and sister. We would argue, in light of this, that it would behoove us to view Genesis 1 and 2 not only as a marriage but also as a prototype for God's kingdom society, how his people—man and woman—will live and work in his kingdom on earth. It appears God's design for governing His creation is man and woman in partnership—mutuality in the home, church, community, and world.

With that lens let's view Genesis 2:24-25 (ESV): "Therefore a man shall leave his father and his mother and hold fast (cleave) to his wife, and they shall become one flesh.[20] And the man and his wife were both naked and were not ashamed."

Cleave (*dabaq*) means to be welded or glued. Genesis 2:24 refers to a relationship between man and woman, but later we see it's used in reference to the Israelites clinging to their God (Deuteronomy 13:4) and in Ruth (1:14) where two desperate women cling to one another for their existence. God's people are to weld to God and to each other; we need that kind of relationship to accomplish the task the Creator gave his *imago Dei*. "One flesh" also points to this concept of interdependence. The author of Genesis points out that woman was literally made out of man's flesh (his rib); they are indeed of one flesh. The term "one flesh" also connotes that just as our bodies are one whole entity and cannot be divided into pieces and still be a whole, so it is with God's people, the body of Christ. Jesus used this word in John 17:11: "Now I am no longer in the world, but these are in the world, and I come to you. Holy Father, keep through your name those whom you have given me, that they may be one as we are one." Jesus continued his prayer. "I do not pray for these alone, but also for those who will believe in me through their word, that they all may be one as you, Father, are in me, and I in you; that they also may be one in us that the world may believe that you sent me" (John 17:20-21). Jesus' reputation in the world is related to our relationships with each other. Paul also spoke of oneness in the body of Christ in Ephesians 2:14-16 and Galatians 3:28. Cleaving and oneness are not solely marital concepts; they also reference the body of Christ in relationship to God and with each other.

The second part of the verse, "Adam and his wife were both naked, and they felt no shame," refers to physical nakedness, but it's more than that. Man and woman were naked with one another spiritually, emotionally, socially, economically, psychologically, etc. What we see is vulnerability between the genders. Dr. Beverly Harrison, a world-renowned scholar on Christian social ethics, calls vulnerability the willingness to be deeply affected by another. Brené Brown, author of *Daring Greatly* and a sociologist and expert on vulnerability, defines vulnerability as "uncertainty, risk, and emotional exposure."[21] The root of the word is from the Latin *vuln*, which means "to wound, capable of wounding, open to attack and damage."[22]

Andy Crouch in his book, *Strong and Weak: Embracing a Life of Love, Risk and True Flourishing,* asserts that flourishing happens best when there is high authority (the ability to act in meaningful ways) and high vulnerability (exposure to risk, open to wounding). Crouch argues that God himself demonstrated this truth at Creation. He spoke and creation flourished, and he also put himself in a place to be wounded by his very own creation. Ponder that concept. And Jesus modeled high authority and high vulnerability when he hung naked on a cross. God has passed down to us this model. Genesis 1 and 2 depict humanity as having the ability to act in meaningful ways, and in Genesis 2:24-25 we see humans were also willing to be deeply affected by others (high vulnerability).

When we ascribe that women, by God's design, are more nurturing, relational, and receptive and therefore more suited for the home, we push women towards vulnerability and away from authority. Likewise, when we teach that men, by God's design, are more assertive, rational, and analytical and therefore more suited for leadership, we push men away from vulnerability and towards authority. In the Garden, God acted with both high authority and high vulnerability as did His image bearers. Therefore, when we expect women to "hold back" or raise men to resist being vulnerable, we reduce God's intentions for his image bearers as full participants in His world.

It's been said that the Jewish people have suffered more persecution than other people groups because they are God's chosen people. In Genesis 3, we read where Satan tempted the woman. In Matthew 2, King Herod killed every male child under two. And in Revelation 12, the dragon awaits the delivery of the child (the nation of Israel). If this is true (and it's debated), then we could deduce that much like the nation of Israel, God's team of man and woman together is dangerous to the evil one. I wonder if the devastation we witness against women and girls—war rape, domestic violence, rape on college campuses, child brides, bride burning, sex trafficking—has something to do with evil at work keeping God's team at war with each other.

Easter Sunday when Jesus arose, he changed things. Jesus reversed the curse. He set into motion full and total restoration of God's creation—God with mankind, the self, each other, and the created world. Jesus said, "The Kingdom is at hand," and yet it is not fully here yet. However, as we live in-between, we live as new creations. We are men and women restored to God and each other. Post-resurrection, our story is that we, God's kingdom agents, are to rule and subdue together in God's kingdom on earth. I'm not ignoring that brokenness is present and corruption exists. However, the Church is called to live the grand story of the Scriptures, and Jesus said we are new creations, resident aliens in this world. Unfortunately, our old soundtrack simply makes us a better version of a broken society rather than new creations. We need a new tune to that old song, one that invites collaboration and calls all people—men and women—to the front line of God's kingdom society. The broken world we live in desperately needs us to sing on key. **It's time to sing a new tune to an old song. Let's do this together!**

> *We need a new tune to that old song, one that invites collaboration and calls all people —men and women— to the front line of God's kingdom society.*

*Chapter 3*

# Relationships in Ruin

My husband and I (Sue) will often send each other humorous pictures and videos to brighten up the day. My husband is an electronics engineer, so I had to send him this one I found on Facebook:

*The oldest computer can be traced back to Adam and Eve.*
*Surprise, Surprise, it was an Apple!*
*But with extremely limited memory*
*It only had one byte. Then everything crashed.*

That sums up what happened to the beautiful relationships that God planned and for which we were created. The Creation story provides us the foundational understanding of our life as image bearers. One of the characteristics of this image is that we were created for and to be in relationship. In the Creation account God placed us in three important relationships: with Himself, with each other, and with creation. Each of these relationships was meant to be good and fulfilling. In the Fall, they were all corrupted and marred by sin. Read the

Genesis 3 account and ponder what was lost that day and how our relationships were forever changed. Do you see the shame, the hiding, the blame, and self-protection? Do you see the domination, pain, strife, harsh labor, and division? The results of the Fall are horrendous. Genesis 3 is Exhibit A, the prototype of the brokenness that infects all relationships in society—a deep rupture between God and us, between each other, and with creation. This is not what God intended for his image bearers. But that is not the end of the story. From this point on, what we see in the narrative of the Scripture is God redeeming these relationships, all of them.

Between Genesis 3 and the Gospels, the population on earth increased, and the relationships created in the Garden grew in number and complexity. These relationships were formalized and became the social systems and institutions of larger complex societies. They grew into religious systems, political systems, family systems, and economic systems. As these relationships grew in complexity, sin within these relationships became complex and institutionalized in societies as well. This systemic sin is expressed in the domination and exclusion of people from the benefits and resources offered in societies. It is expressed in things like economic oppression, war, racism, poverty, slavery, child sacrifice, and worship of idols. These sins are justified by beliefs and ideologies that promote and reinforce the idea that one class of people is less than human, less valuable, and less worthy. It is easier to enslave or humiliate a class of people than to enslave a human created in God's image.

*It is easier to enslave or humiliate a class of people than to enslave a human created in God's image.*

Jesus came to restore the relationships that were ruined. He came to break the bonds that enslave us as individuals and as communities. He came to destroy the barriers and divisions that exclude people from enjoying the fullness of creation and each other. He came to make us a people, His people, all of us, no matter what gender, ethnicity, or class. He did not destroy the social structures that were a part of his society, rather he demonstrated a new way of being the people of God within these institutions. In order to understand the new kind of relationships that Jesus introduced in his teachings, we need to spend a little time understanding social systems and how they can be used to dehumanize, dominate, and exclude. So, the next section will be a bit of an anthropology primer, defining concepts that we will use throughout the book. Then we will look at how they apply to the world in which Jesus lived.

### Structure, Status, and Roles

We were created for relationships and cannot live without them. We cooperate on a daily basis to provide food and necessities for ourselves and for others. We socialize children so they will know how to behave around others. We search out emotional and spiritual support from others. In smaller societies where people know each other's name, most of these needs are met by family members or other extended family. Everyone participates in gathering food, socializing children, providing emotional and spiritual support. Tasks are given to those who have the gifts and talents to meet specific needs. Some labor may be divided into basic categories of age and gender because of age-related capabilities, but these are flexible and vary between cultures.

As the population grows, society becomes more complex, and individuals begin to have more specialized roles. The basic relationships that were formed in the Garden become complex institutions that remain in place beyond the life of the individuals who participate in them. Within these institutions, people no longer relate to each other as persons but rather relate to each other based on relative position in these institutions. For instance, God becomes embedded in a religious system, and we relate to Him

*We are no longer just individuals, but we now belong to categories based on our status or social position within these structures*

through people with the specialized roles of priest, elder, or pastor. Think about how we refer to people in our economic systems. Those who buy a product are called consumers; those who work to produce them are called labor. We are no longer just individuals, but we now belong to categories based on our status or social position within these structures—priests, lay people, consumers, labor.

Status is defined sociologically as one's position in society. It can be either achieved (a position that is earned such as doctor, lawyer, or president) or ascribed (social positions with which one is born or over which one has no control, such as gender, age, family, or class). For instance, the children of Prince Charles, William and Henry, are royalty because they were born into the royal line. They didn't have to do anything; this status was ascribed to them at birth. In many parts of the world your ascribed status, the status in which you were born, is most important for determining your place in society. Think of India's caste system. In the United States, we place an emphasis on achieved status. We love rags to riches stories and believe that anyone who works hard enough can achieve his/her goals.

Status often determines social roles in a society. Social roles are the expectations, obligations, and privileges which society or a particular culture assigns to a certain status. Think of it as a job description for a particular role in a corporation. There is often a list of responsibilities and tasks that a person is expected to fulfill. In many jobs, people have regular evaluations to review whether or not they are performing their role according to the parameters set out in the job description. People are rewarded for their fulfillment of their roles, for instance given a promotion or raise.

Social roles are always cultural, and every culture has different expectations for particular statuses. What it means to be a good father, for instance, differs from culture to culture. Although some statuses are human universals (e.g., age, gender, father/mother), the expectations and social roles assigned are always cultural.

In smaller societies where people relate face-to-face and have fewer societal divisions, statuses are often limited to gender and age. They tend to have fewer well-defined social roles and a more-or-less-equal access to resources. Because of this, there is less marked division between statuses, and there is not a wide range of power related to each of the statuses.

In more complex societies, more social statuses are assigned to people, and people often have several statuses such as gender, ethnicity, social class, age, etc. For instance, both of us authors are Caucasian, highly educated women. Cultures assign value and prestige to certain statuses, both achieved and ascribed. As a result, some statuses have more access to resources, positions, and prestige. Segregation in the U.S., for example, limited access to resources to people with the ascribed status "black." And historically women as a category of ascribed status were excluded from certain professions. Some statuses also have more value in society than others. Think about how we react when we meet someone. Does someone's occupation or wealth give us a better impression of them? The more specialized the culture, the more these statuses define who a person is, the roles they can perform, and the value they have within that society.

In complex societies, people often relate to others based on their status in society. For instance, my students don't address me as Sue; they address me as Dr. Russell. Or another example, we blame those _____ (fill in the blank with any category of people) for the problems in society. In the beginning we were created with the status of male or female that reflected the image of God. Because of sin, however, people use status to determine who is "us" and who is the "other." Note that Adam went from saying, "Bone of my bones and flesh of my flesh" to telling God, "The woman YOU put here with me—she gave me some fruit from the tree, and I ate it." (Genesis 3:12) At first woman was "us," and then she was "other."

Throughout history, status has been used to divide, discriminate, and dehumanize people. Since the Fall, the world has been divided into "us" and "them." We include those who are like us and exclude those who are different. Cain's famous line after he killed his brother, "Am I my brother's keeper," (Genesis 4:9b) reflects this division line between him and me, us and them. Throughout history, those with privileged status have used that status to reinforce their privilege and dehumanize others through rules, ideology, and even religion. This was reflected in the attitude about women in the ancient world in which Jesus lived. One of

*Because of sin people use status to determine who is "us" and who is the "other."*

the results of the Fall was the domination of man over women: "Your desire will be for your husband and he will rule over you.²³ This was systemized into cultures as pa- triarchy and reinforced through ideology reflected in ancient texts. In order to understand how radical Jesus' attitude and interaction with women was in his ministry and the restoration of the relationship between

*Throughout history, status has been used to divide, discriminate, and dehumanize people.*

men and women, we need to spend a few minutes discussing the pre- vailing thoughts and attitudes toward women in the ancient world in which Jesus lived.

### *Gender in the Ancient World*

Jesus was born into a first-century Palestine that was already heavily influenced by Greco-Roman thought and culture. In the fourth century BC, Alexander the Great conquered the Persian Empire, which included Palestine.²⁴ From 300 BC–165 BC Palestine was ruled by a series of Greek rulers. Greek language and culture spread throughout the Greek Empire (see Figure 1).

The extent that the average Jew adopted Greek culture is debated by scholars. However, the influence of Greek culture was experienced throughout the Mediterranean region in many ways. First, the Greek language was spread throughout the region, becoming the lingua franca, the common language. Everyone who desired to participate in political and economic life learned Greek as a second language. During this time, the Hebrew Bible was translated into Greek, and this translation, the Septuagint, became the Scriptures for Jews living in regions outside of Judea.

Figure 1: The Greek Empire under Alexander the Great

Along with the language, Greek religion, culture, and education spread throughout the region. During this time, Greek philosophy became accepted as representing a way of life.[25] Although history records prominent women in the Greco-Roman world, Greek writers provide insights into the prevailing Greco-Roman attitude toward women in Jesus' world.

Homer is considered to have laid the foundation of Greek tradition and was prominent in Greek education and religious thought. He had a pervasive influence on Greek philosophical development.[26] One of the prominent themes in his writing and one that permeates Greek thought is the idea that women are inferior to men. In Homer's widely read work *The Iliad*, women are viewed as possessions of men or are portrayed as the cause of suffering and conflict.[27] They were also portrayed as inferior as depicted in a scene where Zeus challenges one of his enemies with the taunt, "But now they will scorn you, you are, it appears, no better than a woman."[28] In another episode, Zeus scolds his wife Hera as exercising her "crafty evil wiles" and says her actions are "wretched ill-contriving" for which he will "whip you with blows."[29]

Another ancient writer who was also influential in shaping Greek thought is Hesiod. He also paints an unfavorable picture of women. In his poem *Theogony*, he describes the origin of women. According to Hesiod, women are "the beautiful evil"[30] whom Zeus created as a punishment to man for stealing fire. The description of this evil is as follows:

> *For from her is the race of women and female kind: of her is the deathly race and tribe of women who live amongst mortal men to their great trouble no helpmeets in hateful poverty, but only in wealth....even so Zeus who thunders on high made women to be an evil to mortal men, with a nature to do evil.*[31]

According to Hesiod's logic, women are evil creatures who Zeus created as a punishment to men. They were made beautiful so that they were irresistible to man. When a man married, he had to contend with the sorrows that a woman caused him. And as a result of marriage and children, a man will have "unceasing grief in his heart within him do, and this evil cannot be healed."[32] In his writing *Works and Days*, Hesiod warns men, "Do not let a flaunting woman coax and cozen and deceive you: she is after your barn. The man who trusts womenkind trusts deceivers."[33] He also treats women as possessions that men are to obtain along with a house and an ox.[34]

Another Greek writer who had a great influence not only on Greek education of the first century but who continues to influence Western philosophy today is Aristotle. According to Aristotle, woman is inferior to man. He states, "As between the sexes, the male is by nature superior and the female inferior, the male ruler and the female subject."[35] Aristotle's logic is that the soul is better than the body; it is noble and divine. Therefore, "male is better and more divine and the female is the matter."[36] He goes on to state, "The superior should be separated from the inferior, male is to be separated from the female."[37] In Aristotle's thinking, women are considered impotent men. This inferiority of women is also reflected in his reasons why females are born. According to Aristotle, female offspring are born at the beginning and the end of the fertility cycle when the eggs are more poorly developed, and male offspring are born in the prime of life when the eggs are the most developed.[38]

Not only did Aristotle consider women inherently inferior to men, he also taught that they had inferior characteristics. He stated that females are "more mischievous than the male, and (though feebler) more reckless…Males are braver…, whilst the female is more timid."[39] A fuller description of his differences between men and women is as follows:

> The fact is, the nature of man is the most rounded off and complete, and consequently in man the qualities referred to above are found most clearly. Hence woman is more compassionate than man, more easily moved to tears, at the same time is more jealous, more querulous, more apt to scold and to strike. She is, furthermore, more prone to despondency, and less hopeful than man, more void of shame, more false of speech, more deceptive, and more retentive memory. She is more wakeful, more shrinking, more difficult to rouse to action, and requires a smaller quality of nutriment… the male is more courageous than the female and more sympathetic in the way of standing by to help.[40]

Plato, another Greek writer, states this very clearly, "Do you know, then of anything practiced by mankind in which the masculine sex does not surpass the female on all points?" The answer to this question was, "You are right that one sex is far surpassed by the other in everything, one may say."[41] He concludes that because of this inferiority women had no place in the state administration. Plato also emphasizes the need to regulate women because "females are inferior in goodness to males" and "women will use every means to resist being led out into the light, and they will prove much too strong for the lawgiver...women would not as much listen to the mention of the right rule without shrieks of indignation."[42]

The general status of women in Greek literature was that women were inferior to men According to the prevalent thought in the Greco-Roman world, men, as a status category, were more divine and therefore more capable of thought and understanding spiritual matters. Men were also considered nobler, and women were crafty and reckless. The general conclusion of the writers of the ancient world was that women, as a category, were the downfall of men and therefore to be feared and controlled. It didn't matter how smart, strong, or noble she was, a woman was inferior based on her status as "woman." But this was Greek writing and thought, and we need to ask, "How much did Greek thought influence Jewish worldview and ideas about women in Jesus' world?"

*It didn't matter how smart, strong, or noble she was, a woman was inferior based on her status as "woman."*

One example of Greek influence in Jewish thought can be seen in the writing of Philo. Philo was a Hellenistic Jewish philosopher and contemporary of Jesus who used Greek philosophical thought to interpret the Hebrew Scriptures. The Greek attitudes toward women are reflected in his writings. In Philo's interpretations of the Creation account, the first man lived an almost idyllic life. According to Philo, Adam "was so excellent in all good things that he speedily arrived at the very perfection of human happiness."[43] The creation of woman, however, brought disaster upon the man.

In a chapter in which he answers philosophical questions about the creation, Philo responds as to why woman was not also made out of earth. His response was, "This is ordained in the first place so that women might not be of equal dignity with man."[44] He also argues that woman is created second so that she is younger and the husband may take care of her as his daughter."[45] According to Plato, this is why a woman is to pass from the care of her father to the care of her husband. Another reason why women are to remain in the care of men is in his account of the Fall. In describing why the serpent chose the woman instead of the man, Philo responded that "the woman was more accustomed to be deceived than the man. For his counsels as well as his body are of a masculine sort and competent to disentangle the notions of seduction; but the mind of the woman is more effeminate, so more easily caught by the persuasions of falsehood, which imitate the resemblance of truth."[46]

According to Philo, women are slow and have an unstable and rash mind.[47] In Philo's writings, like Aristotle's descriptions of the difference between men and women, he argues that men are superior because men use reason, and women use emotions: "Mind occupies the rank of man, and the sensations that of the women."[48] Philo also taught that women use these sensations to catch a lover and by using her sensations, a woman can easily bring man's mind into subjection to her. The result is that those who have become slaves to this passion will reap the wages of this "miserable and incurable passion." The wages that he describes are those of supporting a family. Philo argued that this makes man miserable and requires him to toil and live a life of incessant labor for subsistence.[49] This Jewish philosopher, like Greco-Roman writers, considered women as a category inferior to men, incapable of reason, and more easily deceived. She was dangerous to men because she could seduce them.

## Women and Judaism

You may be asking, "Does Philo represent the general Jewish understanding of women and their place in Jewish society? How much influence did Hellenism have on people living in Jesus' context, first-century Palestine?" To answer these questions, we turn to the Mishnah, which is a collection of legal rules compiled by Jewish sages and codified around AD 200.[50] Although we cannot uncritically assume exact correspondence to laws in Jesus' context, they do provide a window on the political, social, and religious situation of first-century Palestine. They also allow us to see what influence Hellenism might have had on Jewish attitudes toward women as we examine cases in which the Mishnah differs from the Hebrew Scriptures on which they are based.

According to Professor Judith Wegner, whose PhD is in Judaic Studies, the Mishnah "depicts a society whose central character is the adult Israelite male."[51] One of the areas that there is continuity between the biblical record and the Mishnah is in regard to the legal status of women. The legal status of women in both Hebrew Scriptures and the

Mishnah has to do with who has control of her sexuality; whether it is a father, husband, or Levitical brother. When a women's sexuality is controlled by a man, she is treated as a dependent and has few legal rights. As modern readers we view many of these regulations as oppressive, but in the patriarchal society in which they were practiced, they provided protection for women and limited what men could legally do.[52] Although this placed restrictions on women's right, in the Near Eastern culture they also restrained male dominance. As Old Testament scholar Ron Pierce noted, "Thus though the Torah does not reverse the judgment of male domination (Gen 3:16) it guards and protects within the situation."[53] Similarly, the Torah does not reverse slavery or poverty but rather places restraints on the power that others could exercise over dependent or vulnerable persons.

The Mishnah is also consistent with the Hebrew Scriptures in regard to women whose sexuality was not controlled by a man, such as widows, older daughters, and divorcees. These women were legally independent, had independent rights, and were treated in a more equitable way. They are described as having rational minds, moral sensibility, and competence to own business, at least in the domestic sphere.[54] However, even for these autonomous women, their sexuality excluded them from much of the intellectual and spiritual life of Israel.[55] It is the restriction of women's public participation in the religious and social life of Israel that the Mishnah differs from what is recorded in the Hebrew Scriptures.

> *"...though the Torah does not reverse the judgment of male domination it guards and protects within the situation."*

Hebrew Scriptures provide several positive images of women participating in the public sphere. And as we saw in the first chapter of this book, the Creation story provides a positive image of women as a co-image bearer and partner. There are also stories that highlight the important role women played in Israel's history—Sarah, Ruth, Deborah, and Esther to name a few. The Hebrew Scriptures record women participating in the assemblies, accompanying their husbands when they went on pilgrimages, and participating in the sanctuary. According to Jewish scholar Theodore Friedman, the active participation of women in the religious and social life of Israel in the Hebrew Scripture is the most striking contrast between the Mishnah and the Hebrew Scripture. Whereas the Hebrew Scriptures record women freely participating in public events, the Mishnah emphasizes the segregation of women from public social and religious life.[56]

In the Mishnah there was a distinct separation of the private woman and the public woman,[57] and Friedman explains that respectable women were expected to stay in the home.[58] The Mishnah asserts, "It is the way of a woman to stay at home and it is the way of a man to go out into the market place."[59] Because of this restriction, women were excluded from full participation in the social, intellectual, and religious life of the Jewish community. According to Wegner the exclusion from participating fully in the heart of the Jewish community diminished a woman's level of personhood.[60]

There were several ways in which a woman was restricted from full participation. Women were exempt from performing "every positive precept dependent on time [of year] men are liable and women are exempt."[61] The Mishnah excused women from many religious practices—for instance, active participation in public worship or participation in communal study of the sacred texts.[62] Wegner notes that these exemptions may sound as if they would indicate a positive view of women. However, she argues that these exemptions place the woman's duty to her household above participation in the spiritual and intellectual life of Israel. Exempting a woman from public worship implies that a woman's economic function is higher than her intellectual and spiritual development. Although she could do these tasks voluntarily, in reality this marginalized her in the spiritual life of the community. Those who are required to perform the duties of their religion—i.e., men—are the true core of the religion, the keepers of the tradition. Furthermore, in some cases fathers were actually discouraged from teaching their daughters the Torah. One rabbi claimed that a father teaching his daughter the Torah would encourage her lust.[63]

Examining the commands that the Mishnah required a woman to follow also emphasizes her inferior position in the religious life of Israel. There were only three sets of commands women were required to obey without exception. These commands were about menstrual separation, the dough offering, and the lighting of the Sabbath lamp.[64] So, the question arises as to why these regulations are obligatory and others are optional for women. Wegner notes that these three areas are ones in which a wife's neglect of these duties would cause her husband to transgress.[65] Thus, these commands were not for the women's spiritual and intellectual growth, but they enabled men to perform their religious duties.

Finally, women were excluded from public life because of their sexuality and the danger their sexuality posed to men. Wegner notes that there were three areas in which a woman's sexuality presented a danger to men. First, a women's presence, or by implication her sexuality, could be a distraction to a man's spiritual and intellectual development. "Women were held accountable not only for their own sins but for the lust they awakened in men."[66] This is similar to the attitude of Greco-Roman thinkers who believed that a woman's sexuality could override men's minds.

The second danger that her sexuality presented is that it could cause conflict among men. Because a dependent woman's sexuality was the property of a man, a public appearance might elicit covetousness from another man, breaking the tenth commandment. (Exodus 20:17)

The third danger a woman's sexuality presented to men was her menstruation and men's need for religious purity. The regulations regarding the menstruate needed to be kept in order to protect men from being ritually contaminated.[67] Wegner argues that this fear of pollution kept women out of the public domain. It was deemed better to be on the safe side and exempt women from participation in religious life than to risk men being contaminated by a woman. These three dangers to men meant that women were discouraged from participating in public worship.[68]

The general attitude reflected in the Mishnah regulations was that women had undesirable characteristics that endangered men's ritual purity. Women were not an essential part of the religious community, and their spiritual and intellectual life took second place to their duties to their husband or family. Women also presented a temptation to men and potentially could affect a man's religious participation and spiritual development through their menses and the lust they elicited in men. No wonder a rabbi prayed the blessing three times a day, "Blessed be He who did not make me a gentile, Blessed is he who did not make me a woman, Blessed is He who did not make me an ignoramus."[69]

Although there were a number of women who were given a prominent place in Israel's history, the generalized teachings and laws in the Mishnah pertain to women as a category rather than as individuals. Like the ancient Greeks, the Mishnah reflected the same fear of a woman's sexuality. The laws did not make exceptions for women who had gifts and talents, nor women who were strong and led. Instead, every woman was placed into a category based on their status as a "woman," and then generalizations were made about that category. A person was excluded or included because of a category in which they belonged.

We have seen how ancient writers made broad general statements about men and women and their place and value in society. But who decided which category was good or bad, righteous or unrighteous? Generally, it was determined by those who made up the rules.

*A person was excluded or included because of a category in which they belonged.*

Those with privilege and power used teachings, rules, laws, and, yes, even religion to maintain their privilege. In Greco-Roman society and in first-century Palestine, this privilege was maintained through the cultural values of honor and shame. In order to understand how radically Jesus redefined what was honorable in his kingdom, we need to discuss how honor and shame were defined and reinforced.

### Honor and Shame

Honor and shame in the Greco-Roman world was based on two things. First, it depended on the status categories in which you were born, your ascribed status. These would include things like position in birth order, sex, family name, city of birth, residence, citizenship, inherited wealth, etc. And secondly, it was based on what you achieved, your occupation, earned wealth, position in the broader society, formal education, etc. These statuses were ordered in a hierarchical structure and were the basic organizing principle of Greco-Roman society. Generally ascribed statuses were more valued than achieved ones. For instance, in North American culture some people make a distinction between "old money" and "new money," and typically this distinction is made by those who come from "old money."

The ordering of these statuses was based on the value that society placed on them—what society considered honorable or prestigious. In other words, some positions were considered more honorable or prestigious than others. For instance, in American culture a CEO of a corporation is considered more prestigious than a secretary. As Roman historian Meyer Reinhold notes, "The hierarchical structure of Roman society evolved into one of the most hierarchical and status conscious social orders in mankind's history."[70]

What was prestigious and honorable in Greco-Roman society, what made an honorable person, was defined by the very persons to whom honor meant the most—the upper classes.[71] The rest of the free population in Greco-Roman society was less stratified, but there were divisions based on other criteria. Some of these divisions include citizen versus noncitizen, free versus slave, and head of household versus those in the household. Other statuses such as occupation, residence, family name, and birthplace could also provide honor among the nonelite. Power, education, and moral stature also added prestige to their holders. But it was not just the material elements that marked a person as honorable. It was also the subtle markers: signs of a proper upbringing and education, an aristocratic manner in accent, words, posture, and bearing.[72]

The second thing honor was based on was how well you met the expectations of society for your status. Status came with expected roles and behaviors. Think of the award-winning PBS series *Downton Abbey*. There were specific ways in which the upper class was expected to act, and these were defined by the upper class. Honor was gained or lost depending on how a person fulfilled societal expectations for a social status.

Since a person's honor or prestige was a matter of social perception, status was always on display, and behavior was public and thus could contribute or detract from honor. Holding public office, one's appropriate education and speech and one's moral stature lent prestige or honor to the holder.[73] Status was also advertised in various ways. Roman scholars Peter Garnsey and Richard Saller note that status was linked to wealth and was on public display in the political and religious life of the city. Prestige and honor were demonstrated by the number of clients, the seating at public affairs, and the quality of food and drink that was served to a person at banquets.[74] Competition for honor often subsumed all other competitions and became extremely important to the participants in the competition.[75]

The Jewish world in the first century also was influenced and driven by the values of honor and shame. Many of the same characteristics of honor in Greco-Roman society were also present in Jewish society. Displayed wealth, a good name, and the right family were part of Jewish honor and shame. However, there were characteristics of honor unique to Judaism. In Jewish society, belonging to a particular religious party or sect, maintaining ritual purity, following the law, and participating in temple rituals were areas in which honor was attributed. What was honorable, what was thought to be pleasing to God, was often defined by those who maintained the rules. This system of honor and shame regulated, reinforced, and preserved the divisions between groups and people and excluded classes of people from the religious life of Israel.

## Conclusion

Whew! You made it through a lot of definitions and background information, but we needed to spend time on this discussion to lay the foundation for the rest of the book regarding the redemption of relationships between God and us and with each other. These statuses and categories and the values of honor and shame that reinforced them created barriers between us, but this is the world in which Jesus was born—a world in which there were rules to be followed, honor to be sought and maintained. There were people who were considered honorable and to have favor with God. There were those who were considered *What was honorable, what was thought to be pleasing to God, was often defined by those who maintained the rules.* dishonorable and unrighteous before God just by having the wrong status.

What we will see in the next chapter is that Jesus changed the rules! He redefined who was "in" and who was "out," who was "righteous" and who was "unrighteous." Status no longer made a person honorable in his kingdom. Status was no longer a barrier that included or excluded people from participation in his ministry. Status no longer mattered. Everyone became a part of his people by how they responded to him.

*Chapter 4*

# Relationships Renewed

*19. Now Jesus' mother and brothers came to see him, but they were not able to get near him because of the crowd.*
*20. Someone told him, "Your mother and brothers are standing outside, wanting to see you."*
*21. He replied, "My mother and brothers are those who hear the word of God and do it."*     Luke 8:19-21

There was never a doubt that my older sister and I (Sue) belonged to the same family. We had our father's eyes and nose, our mother's hair. I was three years younger than my sister, but when I walked into a classroom of one of her former teachers, she called me Sheryl, my older sister's name. Even recently when my sister visited me on my birthday, no one had to ask, "Who is your sister?" They just knew. The biological characteristics that we inherited made the family resemblance undeniable.

In the first-century Jewish world, family resemblance came from your lineage, your ancestors. Family lineage defined if you were "in" or "out" and your place in the people of God. Family defined your responsibilities in Jewish society and to others. Family defended one another, took care of one another, and these relationships took priority.

When Jesus' biological family showed up, he redefined his family by describing a new family resemblance. Family resemblance in the new family he was gathering was not based on biology but rather the condition of people's hearts and their response to him. New Testament scholar Joel Green explains this radical transition: "Jesus neither rejects nor praises his physical family; rather, he uses their arrival as a catalyst to redefine in the hearing of his disciples and the crowds the basis of kinship. Kinship in the people of God is no longer grounded in physical descent, he contends, but is based on hearing and doing the word of God."[76]

This was radical! A relationship with God was no longer defined by biology, status, or ritual. Jesus' good news was that those whose status created a barrier from a relationship with God were now included. Those who were at the margins because of their status were now front and center. Statuses that created barriers between people—men and women, Jew and Gentile, slave and free—were now broken. Jesus' good news is that he came to restore our relationship with God and each other, including the relationship between men and women. Those who respond to Jesus are family! The story about Jesus' interaction with Simon and the sinful woman in Luke 7:36-50 highlights the contrast between having the right status and having the right response.

> *Those who were at the margins because of their status were now front and center.*

## He's "Honorable," She's "Sinful"

The central character of the story, Simon, had all the right statuses under the old rules. He was a man and a Pharisee. He would have been viewed as an honorable and righteous person in the eyes of his fellow Israelites. As a Pharisee, he was a respected teacher and practitioner of purity laws. Although many would not be able to achieve his standard of purity, most would have held him in high regard because of it. He was an honorable person in his community and therefore considered righteous before God in others' eyes.

This honorable man invited Jesus over for a meal. It would be easy to assume that Simon was honoring Jesus by his invitation. However, in Greco-Roman culture meals were an important opportunity to reinforce the ranking of honor among the guests. People gained honor by who came to their feast, the kind of meal they served, and what kind of entertainment they provided.[77] Meals were also used to reinforce one's own status by inviting others of lower status to a feast and serving them inferior food and drink. Meals were a way of gaining honor and prestige as well as establishing one's own ranking of honor in social circles. As the narrative begins, we do not know how Simon perceives Jesus.

In contrast to Simon was the sinful woman. We do not know who this woman is or what she has done. All we know is that she had the wrong status; she was a woman and a sinner. The contrast could not be more stark—Simon with the right status, the woman with the wrong status. Simon was at the center of Jewish religious life, the woman at the margins. One is considered righteous in the community, the other considered unrighteous. One was "in"; the other was "out." The contrast in their status brings the contrast in their attitudes and actions toward Jesus sharply into focus. The woman came in and ignoring cultural etiquette went into the room where the men were eating. She began weeping and wiping Jesus' feet with her tears. Then she kissed his feet and poured perfume on them. Her actions were an extravagant display of her humility before Jesus.

Jesus tells a story about forgiveness, but the contrast between the woman's actions and Simon's is the punchline of the story. Whereas the woman wet Jesus' feet with her tears, Simon did not even provide water to wash his feet. Whereas the woman kissed Jesus' feet, Simon did not greet him with a kiss. Whereas the woman poured expensive perfume on Jesus' feet, Simon did not provide oil for his head. By forgoing the social etiquette of a host to a social equal, Simon's actions were designed to humiliate Jesus and put him in his place.

The contrast could not be more glaring. One came in humility to Jesus; the other tried to humiliate Jesus. The dishonorable woman acted honorably toward Jesus; the honorable, self-righteous man acted dishonorably toward Jesus. Jesus makes it clear that it is not a person's status that makes him or her honorable in the Kingdom of God. It is people's actions towards him and others that make them honorable in the Kingdom of God, not their status.

*It is people's actions towards him and others that make them honorable in the Kingdom of God, not their status.*

In this story, it was the woman who had her relationship renewed with God.

Jesus changed the rules! Status no longer made a person honorable or dishonorable, righteous or unrighteous. Status—whether male or female, Pharisee or sinner—neither included nor excluded a person from a relationship with God. Jesus regularly ate with sinners and tax

60

collectors, women, and others on the margins of Jewish religious life.[78] Status no longer divided people into "us" and "them." Those who followed Jesus were now brothers and sisters, God's new family.

Just as status was no longer a barrier to becoming a member of the community, status no longer excluded people from participating in his community. Although Jesus did not say anything explicitly about the role of women or the relationship between men and women,

*Status— whether male or female, Pharisee or sinner— neither included nor excluded*

he modeled it in his own interactions with women. Remember, we learned in Jesus' culture a woman's sexuality was viewed as dangerous, and it kept women on the margins of religious life. However, for Jesus, a woman's status made her neither inferior nor dangerous. Women were not excluded from learning or participating in his ministry. Jesus was not afraid to interact with a woman because of her status as a woman, even if she was considered a sinner, a Gentile, or unclean. We'll look at several examples in which Jesus welcomed women as followers, co-learners, and participants in his ministry.

### Welcomed as Followers

There are several stories where Jesus crossed barriers to welcome women, but we'll only highlight two in which he crosses barriers that were unthinkable in his culture. Perhaps the most poignant story of Jesus' boundary crossing is the story about the woman who was hemorrhaging in Luke 8:40-48. The story is almost hidden within the narrative about the synagogue ruler. Both desperately wanted healing, but that is where the similarity ends. One person came confidently and openly to Jesus. He was a man and a synagogue leader, a person of high status and purity. As a synagogue leader, he was in the center of the spiritual life of his community.

The other is the woman. We don't know much about her, just that she had an issue of blood that would have made her ritually unclean. As an unclean woman, she was at the margins of religious life. Her primary duty was to keep away from others lest she make them unclean. She was excluded from public and ritual life. Two different statuses—one at the heart of Israel's religious life, the other at the margin. However, their status did not matter; both were just people who were desperate and came to Jesus for help.

The story of the woman is particularly moving because not only was she physically sick, but she also was socially isolated from her family, community, and God. She was impure and dangerous to any man or woman because of her potential to make them ritually impure. Yet she had the strength and determination to reach out to Jesus, literally. In a reversal of cultural expectations, her touch did not make Jesus impure, rather he made her pure.

*their status did not matter; both were just people who were desperate and came to Jesus for help.*

Jesus not only restored her physically but socially as well. He called her daughter, an intimate reference, including her as one of his own people.

Another example of Jesus crossing status boundaries is the story about the Canaanite woman in Matthew 15:21-28. In this story we have a woman who would be excluded based on her status as a woman and a Gentile. She was one of "them," both dangerous and unclean. Despite having no claim on a Jewish Messiah, she was persistent in seeking out Jesus to heal her daughter. We don't know why Jesus initially ignored her. But often in the gospel stories when Jesus delayed his answer it is because there is a greater lesson he wanted to teach. Perhaps he was setting up his disciples for a lesson they would not forget.

In the parallel passage found in Mark 7 we learn that Jesus had just clashed with the Pharisee's over their concern that his disciples ate with "unclean" hands. In other words they ate before performing the ritual hand-washing ceremony. (Mark 7:5) Jesus called out the Pharisee's hypocrisy then moved on to a private location where he explained to his disciples what constituted "clean" or "unclean." It was crucial that his disciples, those whom Jesus would leave behind to carry on his work, understood who would be a part of God's new family. The disciples, much like us, struggled to grasp unfamiliar truths, so Jesus set out to give them an object lesson. Jesus and the disciples headed to an "unclean" territory (the region of Tyre) where they engaged with an "unclean" woman—a Gentile born in Syrian Phoenicia. We don't know how long she followed Jesus seeking his help but long enough for the disciples to become annoyed. We'll pick up the story where the disciples were agitated enough with this woman's presence and persistence to ask Jesus to send the woman away.

Imagine the scene. The woman who was "out" persistently asking Jesus to heal her daughter, willing to follow as long as it took to get what she came for. The disciples who were "in" want to send her away because all they saw was a troublesome "other," a woman, a Gentile, a sinner. The standoff continued—the woman seeking Jesus' help and the disciples whose prejudice would stop her. Then Jesus voiced the thought that was on every disciple's mind, saying, "I was sent only to the lost sheep of Israel." (Matthew 15:24) I can imagine a few smug looks on the faces of the disciples. You can imagine them thinking, "That's right Jesus, you're 'our' Messiah." They were sure that the woman would get the message now. Jesus was only sent to the Jews, the ones who by their status as Jews were "in."

But the woman must have sensed something in Jesus' answer, because rather than leaving, she came even closer and knelt before him. Was there something in Jesus' tone that revealed that this was what others thought of Gentiles but not him? We don't know, but for whatever reason she saw his answer not as a rebuke but rather as an invitation. And so, she persisted with her appeal.

Jesus then engaged her in the ancient game of riposte, a word game played among equals. He tossed out the first comment as a challenge: "It is not right to take the children's bread and give it to their dogs." (Matthew 15:26) Here the audience would know that Jesus was talking about giving away what rightfully belongs to the Jews as he was Israel's Messiah. However, rather than taking offense, the woman bantered back, "Yes, Lord, but even the puppies eat the crumbs that fall from their master's table." (Matthew 15:27) I can imagine Jesus being amused at her response and grinning as he granted her request and commended her for her faith.

But can you imagine the disciples' reaction? They had been set up! They had told her to go away because she had the wrong status, but Jesus invited her to interact with him as an equal because of her faith. Her faith drove her to seek out Jesus, and it was this faith that Jesus commended. Her ethnicity excluded her from being a part of the Jewish people, but her response to Jesus made her a co-follower and a co-participant in the family of God.

Many other women became Jesus' followers. In his encounters with women, he treated them as people of dignity and worth. He wasn't afraid of assertive women, nor was he afraid of those who his culture considered impure, inferior, or dangerous. He was willing to confront the leaders and men of his day about their attitude toward women—adulterous women, crippled women, and widows. There were women among those who were fed. There were women who were healed. There were women in the crowds who listened to his teaching. There were women who followed and supported Jesus and his disciples. Women were at his birth, and they were at his grave. It was women who first witnessed the resurrection. Women were a consistent part of his ministry, not only as followers but also as disciples and co-learners in his kingdom.[79]

## Welcomed as Learners

The two examples above demonstrate Jesus crossing status boundaries to welcome those who had the wrong status but the right faith to be a part of his community as followers. It was no longer the right status that mattered but the right response to Jesus and his kingdom. Jesus did not distinguish between men and women in his conversations. He did not exclude women from approaching him, interacting with him, or making requests of him. In fact, he seemed to enjoy assertive, smart, confident women who were willing to engage with him.

> *It was no longer the right status that mattered but the right response to Jesus and his kingdom.*

Jesus never spoke about the roles of women in his community but he welcomed women to speak their minds and to ask questions. He never directly talked about the value and worth of women, but in his interactions he treated them as equals. He treated them as intelligent, capable learners. Rather than considering women as the property of men or as dependent minors, Jesus challenged them to make decisions as independent, moral agents. They were required to make their own choices about who Jesus was and how they would respond to him. He enabled them to move from the margins to the center of the spiritual life of Israel. In his family they were no longer treated as property, they were restored as *ezer warriors*.[80] Let's look at how Jesus welcomed two sisters, Mary and Martha to be disciples and co-learners.

You probably have heard the story of Mary and Martha in Luke 10:38-42 preached several times. This is the story in which Martha was serving Jesus and his disciples, and Mary chose instead to sit with the disciples listening to Jesus. How many times have you heard it preached that it's about being too busy versus having a strong devotional time with Jesus? Although this may preach well, it is not the main idea of the story. Remember the requirements in the Mishnah? A woman's economic role was valued over her participation in the spiritual life of Israel. If given a choice, a woman's priority was meeting the physical and spiritual needs of others rather than her own spiritual needs. Martha's expected role was to serve in the kitchen, welcome guests, and serve the men who were the learners and spiritual heart of Israel. When Jesus came to dinner, Martha was simply performing her expected role. If fact, she was doing an exemplary job.

So, there was Martha in the kitchen doing what she was expected to do, but Mary had crossed the line. She was sitting with the men in the front room. She was neglecting her traditional duties so she could listen to Jesus. She had placed her spiritual life above the physical and spiritual needs of men. She had the audacity to sit with the disciples, and Jesus welcomed her.

Imagine how Martha must have felt with this breach of cultural etiquette, how embarrassed she was. Mary had assumed a role that, up until this point, was reserved for men. Martha was the one who was acting appropriately in her culture and religious system. It was Mary who was out of bounds. Martha, as an older sister, was responsible for teaching her younger sister the role of women in Israel. Her request to Jesus to tell Mary to help her was in essence saying, "Jesus, help me teach Mary her appropriate place which is in the back room with me, not in the front room with you!"

Jesus' response, "Mary has chosen what is better," is not a rebuke to what Martha is doing, but rather an affirmation of Mary's choice to become a learner. Jesus welcomed and encouraged women to sit in the circle with his male disciples. In his response, Jesus indicated that women were co-learners, co-equals, co-disciples. This was extremely radical! Women, who were on the margins of the religious life of

*The relationship between men and women, serving God together, was renewed.*

Israel, were actually invited to be co-participants with men as the people of God. The relationship between men and women, serving God together, was renewed. But Jesus wasn't done with Martha. In fact, he challenged Martha to know him, to really know him.

Martha's journey as a learner continues in John 11:1-44—not in the kitchen but at a grave. Her beloved brother Lazarus had died.

Martha had seen Jesus heal others and knew that he could heal his friend who was sick. But Jesus waited until Lazarus had not only died but had been in the tomb for four days. You have to wonder what Martha thought as each day passed. Perhaps Martha believed Jesus could heal; she had seen that. She could even believe he could raise someone from the dead. But now after four days had passed, that was beyond her scope of experience, beyond her imagination. Her hope died with each passing day.

Have you ever noticed that Jesus tended to give his disciples pop quizzes when the situation seemed impossible and challenged them to do something they thought was impossible? In the boat when Jesus said, "Come," Peter got out of the boat (Matthew 14:28-29). The disciples with two loaves and five small fish looking at 5000 hungry people and Jesus saying, "You give them something to eat." (Mark 6:30-44) Martha with her beloved brother in the grave four days was about to get her pop quiz.

What she believed can be seen in her statement to Jesus: "Lord, if you had been here, my brother would not have died." (John 11:21) Martha had seen Jesus heal others; she knew he could have healed her brother. Perhaps she even had an unspoken accusation, "Jesus, why didn't you come sooner?" But Jesus wanted her to believe not just in what he could do but who he was. Now Martha's pop quiz began.

Question 1: Jesus stated, "Your brother will rise again." (John 11:23) In other words, do you believe I can raise him? Martha knew the right answer for this one. She had heard it all her life and responded, "I know he will rise again in the resurrection on the last day." (John 11:24)

Question 2: Jesus declared, "I am the resurrection and the life. He who believes in me will live, even though he dies, and whoever lives and believes in me will never die." (John 11:25) And then he asked the all-important question, "Do you believe this, Martha?" (John 11:26)

Martha knew the right answer, perhaps the answer she thinks he expects of her, "Yes, Lord, I believe you are the Christ, the Son of God, who was to come into the world." (John 11:27) Sounds good, right? But is this her answer or the expected answer? Is this the answer she knows to be true, or does she really believe this in her heart? So far, she has replied with the answers she had been taught. She answered from her head not her heart, but did she really believe?

Question 3: "Martha, take away the stone." (John 11:39) In other words, do your actions support your belief? Can you imagine what Martha thought in that moment, "What! Did I hear that correctly? Take away the stone!?! He's been in there four days; it's gonna stink!" When Jesus gave his disciples a pop quiz, they often had to do something, something they had never done before that required they trust Jesus at his word. "You believe I am Lord. Well, who do you call upon in a storm? You believe I am the bread of life? Well, let's feed these people." The disciples thought they understood who Jesus was, but Jesus gave them real-life pop quizzes where that faith was tested, deepened, and or challenged to gain a new understanding and experience of who he was. This was Martha's pop quiz: "Do you really believe I am the resurrection? Then take away the stone." Martha's answer? She chose to believe; she chose to believe in her heart what she knew in her head. They took away the stone, and Martha got the biggest surprise of her life! Her beloved brother, whom she thought she had lost, walked out of the tomb.

These are two examples of women who were challenged to learn and act upon Jesus' word. He treated women just as he treated his male disciples. Women were now co-learners as his people. Women were no longer on the margins of their faith, no longer embedded in the actions of their male relatives. Women were now treated as independent agents. They were not "in" because of their status as members of the tribe of Israel or "out" because of their status as women. Like men, they were "in" or "out" because of their own choices, because of their own actions, because of their own obedience to Jesus.

*they were "in" or "out" because of their own choices, because of their own actions, because of their own obedience*

### Welcomed as Co-Workers

Not only did Jesus cross social, cultural, and religious barriers to minister to women and invite women to be his disciples, they became his co-workers in spreading the good news. We have already seen how status, being a women or Gentile, was no longer a barrier for becoming a follower or a learner. Status was also not a barrier for becoming a full participant in Jesus' community as a co-worker in sharing the good news that the Messiah had come. Perhaps the most striking example of this is Jesus' interaction with the Samaritan woman in John 4. Not only was she a woman, but she had two more strikes against her.

First, she was a Samaritan. Culturally and religiously, Jews and Samaritans did not interact. To Jews the Samaritans were a repugnant "other." Jews considered them half-breed pagans. Early in their conversation, the woman highlights this barrier when she says to Jesus, "You are a Jew, and I am a Samaritan woman. How can you ask me for a drink?"(John 4:9).

And second, she was a woman of questionable morals. In the conversation Jesus brought up that she had had five husbands and was now living with a man who was not her husband. We don't know her exact situation. What we do know was that she was at the well alone, avoiding other women and their stares. This woman by her statuses—female, Samaritan, Gentile, sinner—was in stark contrast to the Jews who were considered to be part of God's people—pious, Israelite, males. And yet, it is to this woman that Jesus reveals for the first time that he is the Messiah, and she is the one who spreads the good news about Jesus to the Samaritans.

The dialogue that ensued revealed Jesus' care and concern for the woman. Rather than avoiding conversation with her, he sought it out, initiated it, and was willing to challenge her both intellectually and emotionally. He spoke the truth to her. First, he spoke metaphorically about living water (John 4:10), but before she could understand the metaphor, she had to understand her need for it. It is at this point in the conversation that Jesus confronted her with the truth about herself and her own condition. She tried to move the conversation to a more comfortable discussion, that of religion. Jesus was willing to continue to engage the woman, but he did not patronize her. He spoke healing truth to her. You have to wonder if the final statement of the woman was actually a question, a guess that she was beginning to understand who Jesus was.

> *This woman by her statuses—female, Samaritan, Gentile, sinner—was in stark contrast to the Jews who were considered to be part of God's people—pious, Israelite, males.*

The text reads, "I know that Messiah is coming. When he comes, he will explain everything to us." (John 4:25) And it was here for the first time Jesus clearly revealed his identity, and it was to a woman, a sinful Samaritan woman, the least likely person to be included in God's people because of her statuses. Yet it is to her that Jesus reveals who he is: "I, the one speaking to you, am he." (John 4:26)

"I am he!" (John 4:26) This is the climax of the passage. Jesus was willing to break all barriers and reveal himself to this Samaritan woman—an unclean, unacceptable woman. As New Testament scholar Andreas Köstenberger notes, "In a momentous self-disclosure that is unique to any Gospel narrative prior to Jesus' trials, Jesus now acknowledges frankly that he is the Messiah."[81] Jesus had many conversations with people, but he did not reveal himself as directly as he did to her. In the preceding chapter of the Gospel of John, John recorded a similar conversation Jesus had with Nicodemus. However, in that conversation Jesus did not disclose himself as he did to the Samaritan woman. This is the first time in the gospel that Jesus revealed himself as the Messiah, and he did it to an unclean, Samaritan woman!

The story was interrupted when the disciples returned, so we don't get to hear the woman's response to Jesus. Rather we get to see her response. Upon hearing the good news, she left and told her village about Jesus. The town's people asked Jesus to stay, and many believed in him. Much like the 72 people that Jesus sent out in Luke 10, the Samaritan woman evangelized her village, and as a result both men and women became followers of Christ because of her testimony. This woman, this unclean Samaritan woman, started a revival in her town!

The Samaritan woman was not the only recorded story of women who were co-workers bringing good news about Jesus to others. It was women to whom the angel appeared when they came to the empty tomb after the crucifixion. It was women who believed and went and told the disciples and convinced them to go and see for themselves.[82] In light of Jesus' cultural context, it is remarkable that God chose women to be the first witnesses of the resurrection, the event that changed the ages.

## Conclusion

In the gospels we see that Jesus gathered around him a new kind of people. It was a people not defined by status, ethnicity, gender, class, or religious sect. He defined his people by those who listened and acted upon his word, brothers and sisters in a new kind of family. In Jesus' family, status did not exclude anyone from being his followers, disciples, or

*In Jesus' family, status did not exclude anyone from being his followers, disciples, or co-workers.*

co-workers. Men and women, Jew and Gentile, sinner and righteous, Pharisee and tax-collector were equal participants in his people. Jesus renewed humankind's relationship with God and their relationship with each other—brothers and sisters in partnership to experience and share the good news of Jesus' healing grace.

*Chapter 5*

# The Promise Becomes a Reality

When my (Sue) nephew was young, we used to have a "dumb joke" contest. I have an extensive repertoire of elephant jokes that I would tell him such as, "What do you call an elephant on a train? A passenger!" He would then try and top mine. One of my favorites was, "What happens when ducks fly upside down?" "They quack up!" I think this one stuck with me because it applies to how we often view the Kingdom of God.

Many times when people talk about the Kingdom of God they call it the "upside down" kingdom. The teachings of living in the Kingdom of God seem so radical that they seem completely opposite from how we have learned to live in our society. Our world says to hate your enemy; Jesus says to love our enemy. Our world says to accumulate all you can; Jesus says don't worry about what you will wear or eat, rather seek me first. I could go on with many other examples. But it does seem radical doesn't it? However, in his book *The Divine Conspiracy*, theologian Dallas Willard presents the case that the Kingdom of God is not upside-down living, but rather right-side up living. He argues that the kind of relationships that Jesus teaches about in the Kingdom of God are the life we hunger for, the kind of life we were created for.[83]

*No wonder we feel like the world is "quacking up."*

The Kingdom of God is right-side up living! It's the world that is upside down! No wonder so many people are tired and weary; they have spent their whole lives living upside down. And you know what happens when ducks fly upside down. No wonder we feel like the world is "quacking up."

The gospels record what Jesus taught about this new way of living, restoring our relationship with God, others, and creation. They also show us the new kind of people he was gathering, a group based on a person's response to Him, rather than his or her social status. Statuses such as ethnicity, class, and gender neither gave people an automatic inclusion into the people of God, nor did they exclude people. Jesus inaugurated God's Kingdom through his life on earth. He overcame evil, forgave people's sin, healed people, taught people how to live a new way—God's way, the way they were created to live in relationship with Him, with each other, and with creation as His image bearers.

The book of Acts continues Jesus' story but now through the work of his followers who are empowered by his Spirit. As in Jesus' earthly ministry, a person's social status in the world is no longer the criteria for membership. The Spirit becomes the new identity marker of the people of God. All who are members of the people of God are now marked by the Spirit.[84] The coming of the Spirit marked that the new day, the promised day, had come. With the coming of the Holy Spirit, a new age broke into the present. Let's take a look at how Acts describes this new age in history.

## Living Between the Times

Can you imagine how the disciples must have felt during the three days between the crucifixion and the resurrection? Their hopes for a new life were dashed on the cross. Then came the joy of the resurrection. The Messiah was here! In Acts we see the reality of the Kingdom of God lived out in his followers through the Spirit. It records a new age—an age of the Spirit and a continuation of the ministry of Jesus lived out through his disciples.

The introduction to Acts, Acts 1:1-11 gives us some insight how Luke, the author of Acts, is framing the Kingdom of God in the age of the Spirit. In these verses, Luke, provides a brief overview of what is happening in the 50 days between the resurrection and Pentecost and gives several significant clues about what is to come. First, we learn that the resurrected Jesus appeared to the disciples and provided convincing proof of his resurrection. The Greek word that is translated "proofs" is actually a technical term in Greek that means "evidence that requires a response." It is evidence that is indisputable. There was no doubt in the minds of the disciples about the resurrection. Their lives were transformed by it.

Luke also talks about the Kingdom of God. The expectation in the Jewish worldview was that when the Messiah arrived, he would restore Israel, the actual physical kingdom of Israel. A diagram can help illustrate this. The Jewish worldview divided history into two epochs: the present day and the age to come. There are different versions of how these epochs would come about, but the coming of the Messiah would be the turning point in history. The present day would end when the Messiah arrived, and he would usher in a new age, one in which God would restore Israel and the nations would know God through Israel.

This was the lens in which the disciples were interpreting what Jesus was saying about the Kingdom of God (see Figure 2).

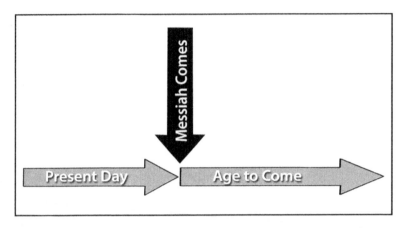

Figure 2: Jewish understanding of the last days

Remember the request that James and John's mother made to Jesus? She asked Jesus that her sons "may sit at your right side and one on your left side when you are king. (Matthew 20:21) She wanted her two sons to sit in positions of honor and prestige in what they thought would be Jesus' earthly kingdom. The disciples thought along the same lines. When Jesus spoke of the Kingdom of God, they were thinking of a physical kingdom wherein Jesus would free them from the Romans who currently occupied their land. They would rule over the people with Jesus when he was king.

So, imagine the disciples' expectations as the post-resurrection Jesus talked about the Kingdom of God. They hadn't expected that the Messiah would be crucified, buried, and resurrected, but he had and was now among them. Thus, their question to Jesus was not totally out of line in Acts 1:6, "Is it now the time when you are going to restore the Kingdom of Israel?" According to their worldview, Jesus the Messiah would now usher in the new age and restore Israel.

The next few verses anticipate a new time, an age of the Spirit. There are three aspects to this new age. First is that they would be receiving the Holy Spirit. The Spirit is not a new concept; the Spirit was given at different times to people in the Old Testament. However, Acts describes the Spirit taking on a whole new function in this new age. Second, they would be witnesses to not only Judea but to those who were not ethnic Jews. Much of the book of Acts reveals how the Spirit incorporates new people into the people of God. And finally, the Messiah would return at the end of this age. So now instead of just two epochs (the present age and the age to come, divided by the arrival of the Messiah), there was a new age—an age between the two epochs, an epoch between the times. It is the age of the Spirit in which the future has broken into the present (see Figure 3).

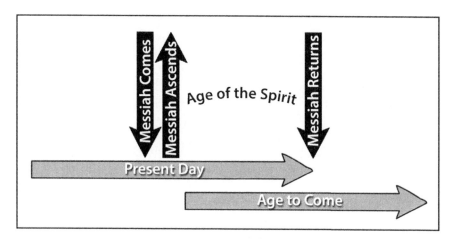

Figure 3: The New Age established by Jesus

### The New Age Has Come!

Imagine being with the disciples waiting for the Spirit Jesus had promised. Luke specifically records that not only the apostles but also women were there among the 120. They were all together, this new community, praying and waiting for the Spirit. In the Old Testament prophecies the pouring out of the Spirit would mark the beginning of the "age to come" and the gathering of Israel. They knew about the Spirit but had not experienced it. Then suddenly the Spirit arrived, not quietly as we might imagine, but with the "sound of a violent wind." They were filled with the Spirit and spoke in other languages. All that Jesus had promised had come to pass. They were excited. It was noisy, and other people, God-fearing Jews from around the Roman Empire, heard the excitement. They each heard people speaking in their own language and asked, "What does this mean?"

The Spirit was here, poured out upon men and women, young and old. The event promised in the Old Testament was now happening. The Spirit was here; the new age had come! And it was the prophecy in Joel 2:28-32 that Peter uses to answer their question, "What does this mean?"(Acts 2:16-22) However, there were significant differences between the Old Testament visions of the coming of the Spirit and the new community that was formed by the arrival of the Spirit at this time. The new people of God would be a community in transition, a community between the times, living in liminality. They were receiving God's promises of the age to come yet there would be a future completion of the promises, too. Peter made several modifications to the Joel quotation that highlighted the "between-the-times" nature of the new community.

The first modification was the addition of ἐν ταῖς ἐσχάταις ἡμέραις, or "in these days."[85] Peter made a direct connection between what was happening at Pentecost and the Day of the Lord. New Testament scholar Craig Keener notes that the phrase "in the last days" was a biblical phrase for the restoration of Israel which was fixed in eschatological time, the end of history as we know it.[86] Luke's narrative indicates that this new age, the messianic age, had dawned with the resurrection of Jesus, but the language in Joel also pointed to a future time when the end of history would become a reality.[87] This outpouring of the Spirit indicated the in-breaking of the Day of the Lord, yet it was not fully consummated. Keener observes, "Peter's last days fits the expectation that the disciples had entered an interim era between the first and second comings of the Messiah, called to testify to the nations by the eschatological gift of the Spirit."[88] During

> *The new people of God would be a community in transition, a community between the times, living in liminality.*

this interim era, the community was "between the times," experiencing the promises of God but waiting for their future completion.

Second, the Spirit became a new identity marker for people in a new community. The Spirit fell equally upon members of each of the basic statuses within the ancient world: men, women, young, old, slave, and free.[89] Keener states, "Joel's prophecy declared the eradication of any gender barrier in the Spirit of prophecy."[90] Just as Jesus had redefined who was a member of the people of God, Mattias Wenk observes that Pentecost represented the fulfillment of Luke 3:16 when the conditions for membership in the people of God were redefined. He concludes, "Another major purpose of Peter's quote is to serve as a description of the prophetic community as the renewed community in which the people who have no status in this world are given the highest recognition by God being accorded the long-hoped-for Spirit of prophecy."[91] Theologian Gerhard Lohfink comments on this new community:

*In Joel 3 it is the Spirit who creates the new order. The new community, which exceeds all purely inner worldly possibilities, can be accomplished only through the abundant eschatological gift of the Spirit. Only in the Spirit is it possible to dismantle national and social barriers, groups' interests, caste systems, and domination of one sex over the other. Religious and social dimensions simply cannot be separated from one another. What happens 'before God' in the realm of faith has immediate social consequences in the church. The people of God, the church as the Body of Christ, is a social reality.*[92]

Third, the Spirit marked a new universal identity of God's people that transcended but did not erase any other social identity.[93] The people in the audience who heard Peter's speech were Jews who lived throughout the Roman Empire and beyond. However, each heard the same message in his or her own language. Three times this is emphasized. People did not lose their ethnic identity but were united in the Spirit within their ethnic statuses. The people of God were now marked by the Spirit as the key factor of identity for membership in the renewed people of God. Membership was not marked by social status, such as gender, ethnicity, class, etc., but by the Spirit. However, they remained in their social statuses.

> *They did not lose their statuses, they were to live out new relationships within their statuses.*

As New Testament scholar Aaron Kuecker observes, "Not only does the outpouring of the Spirit eliminate barriers in the community based on ethnic boundaries, it also eliminates barriers based on other social status."[94]

The remainder of Acts focuses on the incorporation of people into the new people of God, regardless of their statuses. The book of Acts highlights the incorporation of people from different ethnicities, social classes, and genders with all becoming part of the same community through the Spirit. Men, women, rich, poor, Roman, Jew, slave, and free all become members of one community through the Spirit.

In summary, the coming of the Spirit marked two events. First, the Spirit initiated this new community, which was a community in transition between the times. The restoration had begun, but it was waiting for a future completion. Second, people become a part of this new community through their relationship with Jesus, the exalted Davidic Messiah who sent the Spirit. Those who believed in Jesus were incorporated through the Spirit into the new community in which status no longer defined membership or relationships between people. They did not lose their status markers, but they were to live out these new relationships within their structural statuses.

*This dual identity, in-the- Spirit and at the same time in-the-world, is the key to understanding the restored relationships between men and women today —this relation shift.*

This dual identity, in-the-Spirit and at the same time in-the-world, is the key to understanding the restored relationships between men and women today—this relation shift. Many of the debates about gender and gender roles emphasize one aspect of living in a community marked by the Spirit. One side emphasizes the equality that is found in the Spirit and argues that statuses no longer matter in the new community "in Christ." In other words, they emphasize that there is neither Jew nor Gentile, male nor female, slave nor free; statuses no longer matter. The other side emphasizes the verses in which Paul seems to reinforce particular ordering of different statuses. However, we suggest that the emphasis of Scripture is how to live in these new types of relationships with each other within our cultural context. To help us visualize how this fits into the broader biblical context, we introduce an anthropological model that provides a framework to understand the social relationships in the age of the Spirit. We believe this framework moves us beyond the impasse of roles to understanding our relationship as brothers and sisters in Christ.

### A New Lens for Living Between the Times

The framework we introduce is a framework that demonstrates how we can live our new in-Christ relationships within our social statuses, but we need to give you some anthropological background to this framework. This framework uses principles that were discovered and developed by anthropologists studying rituals called "rites of passage." In rites of passage, individuals change their status or position in society. These types of rituals are used to celebrate the birth of a child, adolescence (the transition of a child to adulthood), marriage (from single to couple), and death. Anthropologist Arnold Van Gennep studied these rituals and discovered that they all had three stages. First, there is a separation from former statuses. People going through the rite of passage are separated from society and their structural roles and obligations. The second stage is a period of liminality, a stage in which someone is between and betwixt statuses. For example, they are considered neither children nor adult, single nor married, etc.

In many cultures during the liminal state, individuals are in seclusion and receive instructions on how to perform the obligations and duties of their next status. Finally, there is their reintegration or "reincorporation" into society in which the individual is introduced in their new status (see Figure 4).

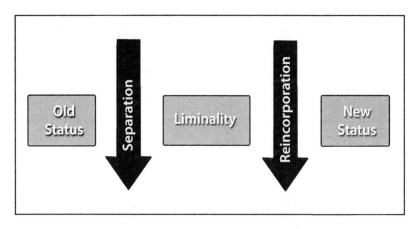

Figure 4: Three stages of rites of passage

We'll use the North American marriage ritual to illustrate these three stages. My (Sue) husband and I were both single adults working in careers when we met. We filed single tax returns, had our own healthcare, etc. We had no legal obligations or rights involving other adults. Our social status in the broader society was that of "single adult" (see Figure 5). After several months of dating, on the shores of the South China Sea, David asked me to marry him, and I said yes. That ritual moved us out of our status of "single" to that of engaged couple, a liminal stage. We were not yet married, but we were no longer single; we were between recognized social statuses in society. We were in liminality. This period was a time of transition where we went to premarital counseling and had talks about finances, children, careers, etc. It was a time of learning more about one another and preparing for marriage.

And then the day arrived! Friends and family came and witnessed our commitment to one another. The end of the marriage ritual had two important steps. First, at the end of the ceremony the pastor said, "By the power invested in me by the state of California, I now pronounce you husband and wife." It was at this moment that we changed status from single to married. But the transition was not complete until the pastor reintegrated us back into society in our new status. The final act of the ceremony was when the pastor turned to the audience and said, "I now introduce to you Mr. and Mrs. David Russell." This ended our period of liminality. We were reincorporated back into society with a new status—married with legal rights and obligations as a married couple (see Figure 5).

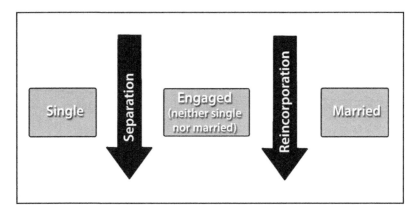

Figure 5: North American marriage ritual

Okay, hold on as we go a bit deeper. We suspect this is new information and may even seem disconnected to the discussion of the role of men and women, but in fact, it's key to unlocking a new way to view this debate. So here we go.

Another anthropologist, Victor Turner, expanded on these concepts specifically exploring liminality (the in-between stage). One of

the most important aspects of his study for our discussion is that Turner contrasted the relationships of people in the liminal state with the
relationships between people in structure. First, we need to understand
what Turner meant by structure. Structure, according to him, is the
working arrangements of society based upon people's statuses and the
ordering of those statuses for a given purpose.[95] In other words, people
in structure relate to one another based on the rules, obligations, and
roles assigned to their social status.[96] In structure, people behave in
ways clearly defined by norms and standards based upon position or
status. Our status also gives us membership into certain groups, which
define our access to resources and the people from whom resources
can be obtained. Okay, you may need to go back and reread that one
more time. Drink in the concept—this is the state of God's people pri-
or to the arrival of Jesus and the coming of the Spirit. People belonged
to the people of God because of their status based on their lineage. Let
me give you an illustration that might help you understand how structure defines our relationships.

When I (Sue) teach in the seminary, I am not just Sue. I am Dr.
Russell and I have certain roles that I need to fulfill, such as teacher,
mentor, advisor. My students, fellow faculty members, and adminis-
trators relate to me based on our statuses within the institution and
the roles we are expected to fulfill. There is also an ordering of our
statuses. I report to my dean, who reports to the provost, who reports
to the seminary president, who reports to the Board of Trustees. This
ordering of statuses within a structure shapes the kind of relationships
I have with people within the institution. For instance, I may feel free
to walk unannounced into the office of one of my faculty colleagues
and chat about my day or my colleague's recent travels, but I would not
do that with the president of the seminary. Our statuses define how
we relate to one another within structure and in many cases define

the kind of relationships we can have with one another. Statuses in structure tend to divide people based on the position of those statuses within a structure.

In contrast to structure, people in liminality are characterized by what Turner calls anti-structure.[97] Anti-structure is the absence of social statuses and roles. In liminality, people are no longer defined by their former structural roles and status. They are just individuals. I am no longer Dr. Russell; I am simply Sue. People in the liminal phase relate to each other as persons without the structural differentiation of status. In other words the social obligations, roles, and behavior that are defined by structure are exchanged for personal relationships between people.[98] People in liminality relate to people as just people. The relationships that are formed in liminality are what Turner referred to as *communitas*. Turner describes this as "the instant mutuality when each person experiences the being of another without the structural social differentiations."[99] It is in lim-

*Statuses in structure tend to divide people based on the position of those statuses within a structure.*

inality that people relate as equals, or as Turner explains, "Communitas is when individuals, although differing in mental and physical endowment, are nevertheless regarded as equal in terms of shared humanity."[100] Turner uses communitas to describe the intense comradeship and egalitarianism experience in liminality in which "personal, structural distinctions of rank and status disappear."[101] Another characteristic of communitas is that people often refer to each other as siblings or comrades of one another.

Although communitas was originally used to describe social relationships within rites of passage, Turner, in particular, expanded the use of the term to describe the social relationships of groups in liminality. Many groups experience liminality when they are removed from society for periods of time. Think of the kind of relationships that are formed during church retreats, military boot camps, or even short-term missions trips. In these spaces we often experience strong intense relationships because people are in a liminal space and are relating as fellow travelers outside their normal structural statuses and roles. We all have experienced this at some point in our life. I experienced this when I (Sue) started my third doctoral program at UCLA. When I sat in class with my peers, it didn't matter how many degrees I already had; I was just Sue to my classmates. I had to do the same reading, write the same papers, and take the same exams as everyone else.

The early Christians experienced this kind of communitas as brothers and sisters in Christ. They understood that they were living between the times and shared a common identity in the Spirit. However, a key difference that sets the early Christian communities apart from other groups in liminality is that they were to live these new types of liminal brother-and-sister relationships within their structural roles and statuses. Whereas many groups experience communitas for a short period of time while separated from society, early Christian communities understood they were living

*The social dimension of living between the times is living brother-and-sister mutual relationships within our social statuses.*

between the times, living this out within the structures of society. This is the social dimension of living between the times; living brother-and-sister mutual relationships within our social statuses.

This is where we find ourselves right now, living in-between the times—you and me (the church) living liminality within our social statuses. In the debate about gender in the church, one side emphasizes the "already" aspect of our kingdom relationship, the liminal equality we find in the new time. The other side emphasizes the "not yet" aspect of relationships that are bound by status and social roles. In actuality it is not an either/or but rather a both/and. Both sides can be supported in Scripture, but we suggest that Scripture shows us how to live the "already" relationships within the structural statuses and roles of the "not yet." We'll show how that works as we continue the discussion.

### Three Dimensions of Living In-Between the Times

Now that we've laid the foundation for this anthropological model, let's apply Turner's framework to Paul's writings and see how it helps us understand the relationships between men and women in the home and the church.

Acts provided us a description of the change in epochs that occurred with the coming of the Spirit. Paul's writings reflect this understanding of living in-between the times. Scholars refer to this as inaugurated eschatology, the "already/not yet" aspects of the Kingdom of God. Paul discusses three aspects of this liminality: temporal, embodied, and social. In the church, we are often hear about the first two of these aspects, but the third has often been lacking in our teaching and is what Turner's model helps us articulate. It is the social aspect that gives us a new lens to view the relationship between men and women. We will discuss all three aspects of our liminal life in Christ to show how the social aspect of his inaugurated eschatology is consistent with the other two. Each of the three aspects of inaugurated eschatology shows the three-stage pattern of rites of passage.

The first aspect, temporal liminality, sets the framework for life within Pauline communities. In Pauline theology, the cross marked the start of the new age in which God's rule had broken into the present age.[102] Although the new age had begun, in Paul's understanding it would not be completed until Christ returns.[103] The new age overlapped the old.[104] The overlapping time in which the new age had started but was not yet complete creates what we call "temporal liminality." The cross brought about an already/not yet experience that produced a tension of living in the new age reality while still in the present age (see Figure 6).

| | Old State | Transition | Liminality | Transition | New State |
|---|---|---|---|---|---|
| **Temporal** | Old Age | *Separation • Cross • Holy Spirit • Baptism* | New Age in Old Age | *Reintegration • Death or parousia • Resurrection* | New Age |
| **Embodied** | Flesh | | Spirit in the Old Body | | Spirit in a New Body |
| **Social** | Status | | In-Christ in Status | | In-Christ |

Figure 6: Rites of passage and dimensions of inaugurated eschatology

The second aspect is what we are calling "embodied liminality." Not only did the cross inaugurate the new age within the present age and in doing so transform time, the new age was also marked by the Spirit who indwelt those who were in Christ, thus transforming individuals. Individuals not only lived in liminal time, but they also embodied that liminality. For Paul, those who were in Christ embodied the *eschaton*, the end of the age, through the indwelling of the Spirit.[105]

Although the Spirit was embodied in Christ followers, Paul also understood that they embodied the Spirit within their physical bodies and literally became liminal people. They embodied this already/not yet in the transition between a fleshly body and a spiritual/immortal body. Just as in the temporal aspects of liminality in which the new age had broken into the present age, Paul understood that Christ followers were still bound to the world through their physical body and subject to attacks of the old dominion.[106] However, Paul emphasized that followers of Christ were to use their bodies in accordance with their new life in Christ. They were not to live as if they were still under the dominion of sin and death.[107] Paul wanted followers of Christ to understand that although they had bodies of flesh they had the capacity to live as children of God because of God's Spirit in them. Therefore, as liminal people, they were not to do the deeds of the flesh but the deeds of the Spirit.[108] They were to actively present their bodies for acts of righteousness, thus reflecting their change of allegiance to God and the new domain in which they lived.[109]

The final part of this embodied liminality in Pauline writing was the reintegration to a new status "with Christ." Paul argued that the reintegration to this new status was at the death of the followers of Christ or at the return of Christ.[110] Paul used the hope of this reintegration to encourage followers of Christ to endure their "slight momentary affliction."[111] For Paul, present life was only temporary, a liminal phase prior to his true life in Christ. Paul wrote, "But our citizenship is in heaven. And we eagerly await a Savior from there, the Lord Jesus Christ, who by the power that enables him to bring everything under his control will transform our lowly bodies so that they will be like his glorious body."[112] These three different stages—flesh, spirit/flesh, and spirit/new body—are similar to the three states in an extended rite of passage in which those who are "in Christ" are in the liminal phase until their death or the *parousia* (the Second Coming of Christ) as seen in Figure 6.

We may not have known the scholarly terms, but many of us have heard teachings about temporal and embodied liminality. But what we believe is crucial to the discussion of race, ethnicity, class, and the relationship between men and women is the third and parallel aspect of liminality—social liminality. It is this social aspect (see Figure 7) that is often missing in discussions of living in the already/not yet liminality. Turner's framework of liminality, structure, anti-structure, and communitas provides concepts to highlight the social aspects of inaugurated eschatology. Let's look at this concept in Pauline terminology.

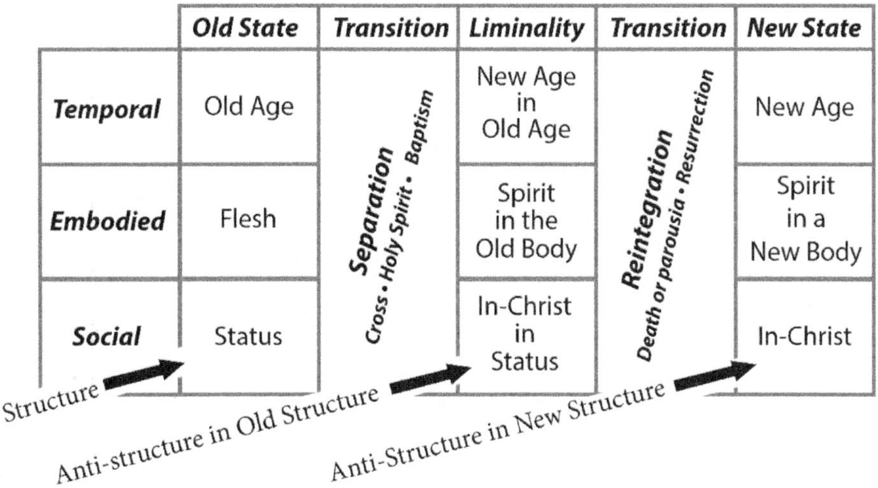

| | Old State | Transition | Liminality | Transition | New State |
|---|---|---|---|---|---|
| **Temporal** | Old Age | *Separation · Cross · Holy Spirit · Baptism* | New Age in Old Age | *Reintegration · Death or parousia · Resurrection* | New Age |
| **Embodied** | Flesh | | Spirit in the Old Body | | Spirit in a New Body |
| **Social** | Status | | In-Christ in Status | | In-Christ |

Structure ➤ Anti-structure in Old Structure ➤ Anti-Structure in New Structure ➤

Figure 7: Living in the social dimension of inaugurated eschatology

First, Paul's teaching is congruent with Jesus' teaching in the gospels that inclusion in the people of God is no longer based on having the right status. Paul made it clear that structural statuses did not qualify (nor disqualify) someone to become a part of the community of Christ followers. Someone became a member of the community through becoming a follower of Jesus.[113] Paul wrote, "For I am not ashamed of the gospel because it is the power of God for salvation to everyone who believes, to the Jew first and also to the Greek."[114]

Second, as we saw in our discussion of Acts, those who are in-Christ have the Spirit. Rather than a community that is differentiated by social statuses, the Spirit was the common identity marker of all Christ followers. Paul wrote, "You however are not in the flesh but in the Spirit if in fact the Spirit of God dwells in you. Anyone who does not have the Spirit of Christ does not belong to Him."[115] This identity transcended other status makers so that the structural statuses of members in the community no longer divided people. According to Paul, people were "baptized by one Spirit into one body."[116]

Third, those who belonged to the in-Christ community were expected to relate in a way that reflected their common identity in the Spirit, as brothers and sisters in Christ. In his writing, Paul not only uses "in Christ" to mark the identity of the individual as a member of the new community but also to articulate the expected actions of people within the new liminal community and the way

> *We are to relate to each other according to our overarching identity of "in Christ"...but to do it within our current social statuses.*

that they were to relate to one another.[117] When Paul wrote that there was neither Jew nor Greek, slave nor free, male nor female, he was not just talking about spiritual equality; he was speaking of how they were to relate to one another, relating mutually as spiritual equals in-Christ.

The final point is crucial. This new in-Christ identity did not erase the status differences of people in the community. However, people were to relate to each other according to the same overarching identity of "in Christ" within their structural status. In other words, we are in social liminality where we are experiencing the in-Christ community mutual relationships, but we have to do it within our current social structural statuses. This is the overarching hermeneutical framework for interpreting Paul's teachings concerning interpersonal relationships within the community as they were lived out in the world. This is crucial for understanding our new relationships as men and women in the home and the church, so I want to emphasize it once again.

Unlike other liminal communities which separate themselves from structure or erase social distinctions, the in-Christ identity marked by the Spirit transcended but did not erase these social differentiations. These new liminal mutual relationships are to be lived in structural statuses and roles. That

*How these mutual relationships are lived out will look different in various cultural contexts.*

means how these mutual relationships are lived out will look different in various cultural contexts. In the next two chapters, we will discuss what living mutually within structure looks like. First, we'll look at the quality and characteristics of relationships within the in-Christ community. Then we will look at how Paul instructed people to live out these new relationships in the structural statuses and roles of their cultural context.

*Chapter 6*

# Siblings in Christ

The cross changed everything. We live in a new time. We are new creations in Christ. We belong to a new community, the in-Christ community. No longer do our statuses divide us, but rather we are united by Christ, marked by the Holy Spirit given to us in Christ. The Spirit in us now distinguishes those who belong to the community and those who are outside the community. Our statuses in the world do not include, nor do they exclude us. Although we remain in our structural statuses, our primary identity in this new community is in the Spirit.

Paul makes it clear that within the in-Christ community, behavior and interpersonal interaction are to be characterized by communitas in which we relate to one another as persons, not according to our social statuses and roles. Paul uses the metaphor of siblinghood to describe what the relationships are to be like in this new community. Even though people do not have the same statuses, nor are we the same, we are to treat one another with the love, humility, and affection of siblings. It is this idea of treating members as siblings that reflects the nature of these new relationships in-Christ.

## Siblinghood of Believers

The most pervasive metaphors that Paul used to describe the interpersonal relationships between members of the in-Christ community were sibling language.[118] New Testament scholar Joseph Hellerman notes that the sibling terminology occurs 118 times in the broader Pauline writings.[119] He states, "The idea of the church as family is ubiquitous in Paul's writing and is, therefore, central to Paul's understanding of the manner in which interpersonal relationships are to function in the communities to which he writes."[120] However, as with any metaphor, there are multiple and complex meanings that can be attached to it. There are three primary ways in which sibling terminology defined the nature of interpersonal relationships in Pauline communities.

First, sibling terminology highlighted the primary identity of in-Christ community members as the basis of their relationships. Lohfink states, "The brotherhood and sisterhood of the early Christian communities were based on the eschatological outpouring of the Spirit."[121] The primary identity of community members was as siblings under the authority of God the Father. Group identity and interaction were no longer defined by status but by the Spirit of Christ.

Second, Paul's use of siblingship reflected the liminal nature of interpersonal relationships that were lived out within structural statuses. There were differences in status among members of Pauline communities; his communities were not homogenous. However, interpersonal relationships between community members were not based on these statuses but on their common identity as siblings in Christ. They were, as New Testament scholar Scott Bartchy describes, nonpatriarchal without being egalitarian.[122] In other words they didn't have the domination of patriarchy, but that didn't mean everyone was equal in status. For instance, there were still rich and poor, but they were to relate to one another as brothers and sisters. Paul's use of sibling terminology was to encourage

*relationships between community members were not based on their statuses but on their common identity as siblings in Christ.*

relationships of mutual responsibility and sharing within the community rather than the competition, domination, and exclusion that were a part of the relationships in the social structure. The early community was not homogenous, but the sibling terminology allowed the community to "embody differences and asymmetrical relationships among members for reciprocal collective actions."[123]

Third, in Paul's time, the usage of sibling terminology not only described social relationships (family), but it depicted day-to-day behavior between siblings. Calling someone by a family relationship was to call upon the social obligations and expectations of family members. Have you ever called a person "aunt" or "uncle" or "cousin" when in fact they were not related to you? They have "family rights," like borrowing the car or getting food out of your refrigerator without asking. These folks are our "honorable kin." We engage honorable kin as if they were our real blood family. This past year when my (Sue) last sibling passed away I was deeply moved when my cousin wrote me saying, "You're our sister, too." She extended an invitation that redefined our relationship from extended kin to nuclear family. This is similar to what Paul communicated when he used sibling terminology. Hellerman suggests that of the total repertoire of relationships in the ancient world, Paul used the sibling relationship because it most closely provided the model for the quality of interpersonal relationships in the community, ones based on bonds of affection and choice.[124] It was mutual affection and love rather than social statuses that provided the basis for interaction and unity of in-Christ communities.

There were several expectations concerning behavior of siblings in the ancient world which were reflected in Paul's writings. First, there was the expectation of generalized reciprocity for both meals and resources.[125] People were to give without expectation of return, and people received without obligation. Second, there was to be an affection for one another that was lived out in respect, honor, and caring for one another.[126]

*It was mutual affection and love rather than social statuses that provided the basis for interaction and unity of in-Christ communities.*

Siblings were also to protect each other from adversaries as well as provide correction in behavior when necessary.[127] Finally, ideal sibling relationships were characterized by harmony and peace.[128] All of these reflected the mutual love and affection that Paul expected of interpersonal relationships within the in-Christ communities. This mutuality, love, and affection are expressed in several ways in Paul's writings, expounding on the life of Jesus and his teachings about the Kingdom of God.

### Mutuality of Liminality

One of the ways Paul expresses sibling relationships is through the language of mutuality. Paul expresses this characteristic through the use of the reciprocal pronoun ἀλλήλων, *allélón*, "one another" in his writings.[129] Like siblings, members of the in-Christ community were to be committed to and engaged with each other in mutual exhortation, care, and harmony.[130] Another New Testament scholar, Volker Rabens, asserts, "This is even intensified by the fact that Paul longs for mutual participation in each other's spiritual life which results in both parties being encouraged."[131] Below are several of Paul's usages of ἀλλήλων:[132]

» Be devoted to one another (Romans 12:10)

» Honor one another above yourselves (Romans 12:10)

» Live in harmony with one another (Romans 12:16)

» Love one another (Romans 13:8)

» Accept one another (Romans 15:7)

» Instruct one another (Romans 15:14)

» Greeting one another with a holy kiss (Romans 16:16)

» Have equal concern for one another (1 Corinthians 12:25)

» Serve one another humbly in love (Galatians 5:13)

» Carry each other's burdens (Galatians 6:2)

» Be patient, bearing with one another in love (Ephesians 4:2)

» Be kind and compassionate to one another (Ephesians 4:32)

» Submit to one another (Ephesians 5:21)

» Forgive one another (Colossians 3:13)

» Encourage one another (1 Thessalonians 5:11)

» Live in peace with one another (1 Thessalonians 5:13)

» Do what is good for each other (1 Thessalonians 5:15)

If you're like me, you quickly read through this list as if you were reading the instructions on an aspirin bottle. No imagination is needed. But to put those words, "love one another," into action require real life and bold movement between people. Speaking encouraging words like "Hey, Sally, I really admire how you treat your daughter" or bearing another's burden like doing Scott's laundry while he battles cancer is real day-to-day life, and in the day-to-day "otherness," we are bound to become more intimate and known by each other. How can you not? Paul emphasized the brother-and-sister relationship and in doing so didn't stipulate its application to be just guy-to-guy or girl-to-girl. It's as siblings so guy-to-guy, girl-to-girl, guy-to-girl. We live in a sex-crazed culture, and some of us have experienced the pangs of infidelity or abuse. The cost is high, but we are called new creations, called to live in faith not fear. To be biblical, we've got to learn a new narrative—Paul's narrative of brother and sister where the "one anothers" apply to all sibling relationships and are to be lived out between sisters, between brothers, and between brothers and sisters. It's a lofty ideal, but theology must be lived in praxis; otherwise it's simply pie-in-the sky thinking.

The mutuality expressed in these commands reflects the ideal of siblinghood. Members of the in-Christ community were no longer to relate to one another on the basis of structural statuses but as siblings of the same family in Christ. They were to "one another" each other based on their common identity in Christ. This did not mean an erasure of these statuses; they continued to have different social statuses. Nor did it mean that all in the community had the same capabilities since people had different spiritual gifts. However, as in other families, their social statuses and spiritual gifts were to be used for the benefit of other members of the family.[133]

### Humility Toward Siblings

Like mutuality, the emphasis on humility in Pauline writings shifted the focus of one's gifts from self to others. In the Greco-Roman world, status, achievements, and gifts were used to elevate oneself in the ever-present game of honor and shame. Humility was antithetical to the Greco-Roman value of keeping or increasing one's honor at the expense of others.[134] Humility in Pauline writing was not submission under the dominion of others, but it was recognition of the value, dignity, and worth of each member of the community regardless of social status.[135] Unlike modern notions, humility was not putting oneself down, but rather the life of humility was choosing a life in mutual submission and of honoring one another.[136]

Paul expressed this call to humility in several ways. One was that people were not to consider themselves more honorable than others based on their status. Paul acknowledged there were different statuses in the Christian communities but wrote that people should not base their relationships on those differences. People weren't to be haughty and set themselves apart based on those statuses. Instead they were to engage with people of all statuses, including those with the lowest status. People were also not to humiliate others because of their low structural status, such as was

*humility was not putting oneself down, but rather the life of humility was choosing a life in mutual submission and of honoring one another.*

happening in the Corinthian church at meals.[137] Nor were they to compare themselves with others. They were not to judge others nor elevate themselves by boasting or becoming conceited.[138] They were also not to envy those whose status was higher.[139]

Another way humility was expressed is that they were not to use their status for their own gain. They were not to be involved in rivalries or competitions for honor, and they were to relinquish claims of recognition and offer recognition to others.[140] They were not to use their status to elevate their own interests but were to consider others and their interests as more important than their own.[141] They were not to be self-seeking, nor to do anything from rivalry or conceit.[142] They were to rejoice in another's honor rather than promote their own.[143] Those who were humble renounced their rights to use status, knowledge, or freedom for self-gain.[144]

The call to humility and consideration of others was both the recognition of status differences within the community and at the same time a way of overcoming status differences by redefining what was honorable within the community.[145] As in Jesus' teaching, Paul did not reject the notion of honor but redefined what was honorable in the in-Christ community. Social capital or status was not something to be exploited for oneself but rather something that was to be used for others. Paul used the greatest example of status being used for others in Philippians 2, in which Paul writes about Jesus, who was the very nature of God (highest status) but used his status for us by taking the very nature of a servant and dying on the cross.

## Love Toward Siblings

Once again Paul builds on Jesus' teachings. Like Jesus, for Paul, love was a central characteristic of sibling-like relationships in the Kingdom of God. Love transcended the limitations of economic, ethnic, gender, and insider/outsider boundaries. Love was the outworking of the new life through obedience to Christ and indwelling of the Spirit.[146]

The love Paul intended was ἀγάπη, "*agape*," which he used to describe how God acted on our behalf through the death of Christ.[147] Thus, the cross was central to Paul's concept of love. Theologian Gordon Fee argues that for Paul "To have love means to be toward others the way God in Christ has been toward us."[148] Paul challenged people to "be imitators of God."[149] Members were to look to Christ's example for their understanding of what it meant to love others in the in-Christ community. They were to "walk in love as Christ loved us and gave himself up for us."[150] For Paul, love was action that was directed towards others and sought the best for them.[151] Love was the core expression of being siblings as members of the in-Christ community.

Sibling love encompassed the other characteristics of the liminal community.[152] Paul's writings about relationships within the community taught ways in which love was expressed and what it meant to be other-centered: to "one another," to have humility, and to treat each other as brothers and sisters. Many times Paul did not list specific actions but rather allowed individuals to be guided by love and to do what was best for others in a particular situation.[153]

In his treatise on love in 1 Corinthians 13, Paul appealed to the Corinthians to use gifts not for themselves but according to agape love so that they served others. As New Testament Professor Michelle Lee notes, "Only when they are used in love do they become useful in building up the church."[154] Conversely, when gifts were not used in love, Paul considered them useless because they divided and caused harm to the community.[155] For Paul, love was

*Love was the foundation for communitas.*

the basis for unity; actions based on self-interest divided the church.[156] Concerning 1 Corinthians 13, Roy Ciampa and Brian Rosner affirm,

"Paul's comments about love are not based on some abstract, context-free meditation on the subject, but on providing a stinging contrast to the behavior of some members of the Corinthian community."[157] Love was the foundation for communitas.

Love in the Pauline community was expressed in concrete ways, too, specifically in guiding the community members' attitude toward possessions. In the Greco-Roman world, people could gain honor by using their wealth for the common good, which generally entailed building public buildings and monuments. (Analogous today would be the Rockefeller Museum in New York or the Getty Center in California.) In doing so, they were acting in their own interests by maintaining or increasing their honor in society. However, in Pauline communities, possessions were not just a means to gain status and honor for oneself but another means that expressed sibling love towards one another. Pauline communities were exhorted to give generously, not only to their own group but also to the broader community of believers.[158]

### Conclusion

One of the most distinguishing features of the early Christian communities was the sibling-like relationships that people had with one another across class, ethnic, and gender boundaries. People were neither the same nor equal in status within the community, but their status neither excluded nor included them. These relationships were not based on the structural statuses, roles, and obligations they had in the broader society but on mutuality, humility, and love as siblings in Christ.

Love rather than self-interest was to mark all relationships of the followers of Christ. Sibling-like concern was to be extended to those outside the community.[159] In doing so, they reflected a new way of living to the world. Jesus said that they would be known for their love for one another.[160] However they were not to live these relationships in isolation. They had to live these sibling like relationships in the real world. We'll examine how that looked in the next chapter.

*Chapter 7*

# Siblings in the World

The previous chapter discussed the new kind of relationships we are to have with one another as members of Christ's family. This siblinghood of the early Christian communities which emphasized mutuality and affection was rare in the ancient world. Although there were organizations in the Greco-Roman world that would promote these kinds of ties, rarely did they transcend gender, ethnicity, and class as in the Christian communities. Furthermore, these types of relationships would only be sustained for short periods or in certain organizations or special locations. What was unique for the in-Christ community is that they were to live out liminal relationships within a very hierarchical, stratified society with rigid divisions between class, gender, and ethnicity.

The uniqueness of the early Christian communities was not that everyone was the same or that they renounced their status. The uniqueness of Christianity is that people are to treat one another as brothers and sisters in Christ within their structural statuses. Bartchy concludes, "The person who had been called was no longer defined as a Jew or Greek, as a male or female, as a slave or a freeman, but as a saint; this 'holiness of Christ' was not a status but a new way of existing in the world under the grace and the command of God."[161] Christ transformed highly stratified, hierarchical communities into ones in which people served one another no matter what their status. Status or privilege was a gift that was to be used for the service and good of others.

*The uniqueness of Christianity is that people are to treat one another as brothers and sisters in Christ within their structural statuses.*

However, some of Paul's writings have been interpreted as reinforcing the hierarchy of statuses, such as seen in passages about husbands and wives specifically in Ephesians 5 and Colossians 3. These passages seem to conflict with statements about the mutuality of the people in the community that we outlined in the last chapter. The concepts of structure and anti-structure provide a framework to reconcile these seemingly contradictory statements. We argue that in these statements Paul is illustrating how sibling-like relationships are to be lived out within the hierarchal Greco-Roman society. We will address each of these structural categories in the order presented in Galatians 3:28.

### Neither Jew Nor Gentile

As we noted in the previous chapters, people from different ethnic identities were incorporated "in Christ" and marked by the Spirit with a common identity. New Testament scholar Bruce Hansen argues that becoming a part of the in-Christ community did not fundamentally change people's ethnic categories, but the in-Christ communities were free of cultural domination and exclusion.[162] In second-temple Judaism and in Greco-Roman culture, ethnic differences were a part of the discourse of exclusion, hierarchy, and domination. As New Testament scholar Kathy Ehrensperger observes, "To be a member of a people other than Greeks or Romans and to adhere to another culture and value system meant to be despised as uncivilized, barbaric, even born to be slaves."[163] To become a member of the dominant culture, people had to become Romanized or Hellenized and lose the distinction of their ethnicity and language. There was no equality for people of a differing ethnic background. Ehrensperger notes, "The hierarchy of peoples was absolutely clear in Greco-Roman culture, and it justified domination of others."[164]

Within Paul's writings, although Jews and Gentiles are one in Christ, they still retained their ethnic and linguistic distinctions.[165] Paul did not ignore these differences. However, people were to live as one within their ethnic statuses.[166] The mutuality and solidarity between people of different ethnicities in Christ challenged

*Paul is illustrating how sibling-like relationships are to be lived out within the hierarchal Greco-Roman society.*

the hierarchical Greco-Roman world filled with the dominating and dominated. In both cases, the Jewish exclusion of Gentiles and the Roman domination of others, the common in-Christ identity challenged both exclusion and domination based on ethnic identity. Members of the early Christian communities did not have to change their ethnic identity nor have a common ethnic identity, but they were to be united in their diversity. They were to express their identity of "in Christ" within their own ethnicity and language.

This means that when we are part of a multiethnic community, things will not always be done our way or to our own tastes. When I (Jackie) worked in a local church, one of my responsibilities was to train other women how to teach the Bible effectively. Our women's Bible study was composed mostly of white suburban women who spoke "Texas" English. However, there was also a group of about 50 non-English speaking Hispanic women from Latin and Central American. One of the Hispanic women, who spoke fluent English, took our training, and afterwards I suggested she be put in our rotation of teachers. But there was concern that the rest of the women wouldn't feel comfortable with her strong accent. I reminded our leadership that these Hispanic women had sat each week listening to white Texas-speaking women and never complained about our accents.

> *Living as a multicultural community means we need to be willing to be uncomfortable sometimes.*

Learning how to live as a multicultural community within the church means we need to be willing to be uncomfortable sometimes. We may not get to sing the music that we like to sing every Sunday, or listen to the speaker that we prefer, or learn about topics that are pressing for us. It requires us to recognize the needs and interests of others and intentionally work to please everyone some of the time. Doing so allows us to learn and appreciate cultural differences and be a unified community with those differences.

## *Neither Slave Nor Free*

Just as Paul did not encourage Jews and Gentiles to change their ethnicity, neither did he encourage slaves to change their condition. However, what Paul advocated was the inclusion and equality of all statuses in Christ. Paul welcomed slaves into the community as equals within the body of Christ, and they shared in the common identity of in Christ. According to Bartchy, Paul saw religious, social, or legal statuses as neither a hindrance nor an advantage with respect to living according to their calling.[167] God had not called them out of their previous statuses but into Christ.[168] For Paul, the statuses of slave and free were meaningless for the relationships of those in Christ. What mattered was obedience to Christ's commands, in other words living anti-structural lives within the structures of their society.[169] However, this did not mean Paul was prohibiting slaves from changing their status.[170]

Although Paul did not directly challenge the institution of slavery, he did change the perception of slaves. Within the in-Christ community, a slave was no longer a thing but rather a person, a fellow brother or sister in Christ.[171] In his letter to Philemon, Paul acknowledged the institution of slavery and the Roman legal right of Philemon to own Onesimus. Although Paul would have liked to have kept Onesimus with him, he left the decision to Philemon. He wrote, "I do not want to do anything without your consent."[172] Although there was implicit acknowledgment of the slave/master relationship, Paul appealed more strongly to the new anti-structural relationship of mutual membership in the body of Christ. Paul wrote to Philemon that he returned Onesimus to him no longer as a slave, but more than a slave, as a dear brother, a member of the in-Christ community.[173] Finally, Paul asked that Philemon welcome Onesimus as he would

Paul himself, reflecting that in Christ there was no difference between free and slave.[174] What is interesting is that Paul did not demand that Philemon free Onesimus but rather encouraged him to treat Onesimus as he would any member in the body of Christ—even while Onesimus remained a slave. However, implied in Paul's letter is the desire that Onesimus would become in the social structure what he was in Christ, a brother rather than a slave.[175]

### Neither Male Nor Female

The framework we have been discussing of living as siblings in Christ within structure also applies to Paul's statements about the relationship between men and women, particularly in marriage.[176] Paul redefined how men and women, particularly husbands and wives, were to live as brothers and sisters within the hierarchal structure of Greco-Roman households.[177] The in-Christ identity and mutual submission made the hierarchical arrangement of statuses in marriage irrelevant. Distinct passages about the relationships of husbands and wives illustrate their consistency with other Pauline instructions of living as siblings in Christ within structural statuses.

In 1 Corinthians 7, Paul wrote extensively about issues of marriage, sexuality, and divorce, addressing both men and women in a balanced way. There were three distinct aspects of marriage that Paul addressed. Within marital rights, the structural expectations of marriage were that women belonged to their husbands.[178] It was the structural role of a wife to fulfill her duty to her husband because her body did not belong to her but to her husband.[179] However, in the new community (the body of Christ), mutuality was expressed within these structural roles. Not only were wives to fulfill their duties to their husbands, but husbands were mutually responsible for fulfilling their duties to their wives because their bodies belonged to their wives. [180] The mutual responsibilities—the "one another" of the in-Christ community—was demonstrated in marital relationships between husbands and wives.

> *The in-Christ identity and mutual submission made the hierarchical arrangement of statuses in marriage irrelevant*

The second way that Paul demonstrates this same kind of mutuality within marriage was in the marital responsibility and choices within mixed marriages—marriages in which one spouse was a follower of Christ and the other was not.[181] In these verses, Paul spoke about divorce, particularly about divorce and choices in mixed marriages. A wife who had an unbelieving husband was instructed not to divorce her husband. In the same way, men were not to force their wives to stay married or convert to Christianity. Once again, Paul expressed the mutuality of the in-Christ community by making the same demands on men as on women. Men were not to divorce their wives, and they were instructed to stay married to unbelievers should the unbelieving spouse desire it. Both men and women had the same obligation to their marital partners. This even-handed mutuality stood in stark contrast to what might have been expected from other writers living in the first century.[182]

Finally, Paul addressed marital choices and service to the Lord.[183] Both men and women were given the choice whether to marry or remain single in their service to Christ. As with ethnicity and slavery, they were to pursue living as siblings in Christ in the context of their present status.[184] Once again, in a society that gave only men the choice in regard to marriage or celibacy, in the in-Christ community there was no difference in choices given to men and women. Both were allowed to determine what was best for them in regard to marriage and service to Christ. As New Testament scholar Gilbert Bilezikian notes, "This text indicates that the early church did not perpetuate in its life the functional differentiations between male and female that were prevalent in its ambient patriarchal society. Men and women were treated as equals in their service in the church."[185]

The final concept examined here is the description of a new way of living as husband and wife within the hierarchical Roman household.[186] Some argue that in these verses the writer is reinforcing the hierarchy and domination of the *pater* (father) over the household.[187] However, this passage must be interpreted using the same framework of living as siblings in Christ within the structures of society. In Ephesians 5:21–6:9, the author addresses the mutual submission of those in Christ in three different role relationships of people with different social statuses in the household: husband/wife, father/child, and master/slave. The structural obligations within the Greco-Roman society were for wives to submit to their husbands, children to obey their fathers, and slaves to obey their masters. However, the emphasis of this passage is how in-Christ members were to live anti-structural, exemplary lives within that structure.

The writer made two fundamental changes to the expectations of the traditional relationship between husbands and wives that reflect this emphasis. First, he provided a new motivation for societal expectations. Wives were not to submit to husbands because of societal expectations and obligations, but rather submission was based on mutual submission and respect between siblings in Christ.[188] For a wife who was a Christ follower, especially if married to someone who was not, this provided a way for her to please Christ within the structural obligations of her household. As a member of the in-Christ community, her conduct toward her husband, whether Christian or non-Christian, was to be Christ-like.

Second, the writer outlined sibling-like mutual submission for a man in his structural role as husband. Paul does not deny that a hierarchy existed but rather describes sibling-like mutuality in the hierarchical arrangement of structural statuses. He reinforces the in-Christ community expectations that those in the privileged status were to use their status for the benefit of others.[189] As a Christ follower, a husband was to use his privilege not in power and domination but in love and service.[190] The actions of husbands and wives toward each other were to reflect the mutuality of members of the in-Christ community and in doing so transform the hierarchical relationship between husband and wife.

*Paul does not deny that a hierarchy existed but rather describes sibling-like mutuality in that hierarchy.*

What we are emphasizing is that Paul is demonstrating how to live mutually within the cultural structures of his context. In the context in which it is written, this passage is demonstrating how to live in a mutual and sibling-like relationship within marriage within that particular culture's hierarchical structure. It is not emphasizing the structure but how to live in liminality within the structure. Because the role relationships between husbands and wives are not the same across cultures, how this mutual relationship will look will vary from culture to culture, but the emphasis is on the mutual relationship. This passage is neither supporting nor undermining any particular structure but rather demonstrating how Christians can relate as brothers and sisters within their structure.

## Conclusion

Often in the debate about gender and gender roles in the church, people emphasize one aspect of the social dimension of living between the times. Some emphasize Galatians 3:28 in which social status no longer included or excluded people from the in-Christ community. However, others emphasize the verses that seem to reinforce status differences of people in the in-Christ community. Understanding that there is an already/not yet social dimension of the in-Christ community reconciles seemingly contradictory statements in Pauline writings. The interpretive framework for social relationships of living as siblings in Christ within the structures of society allows a consistent interpretation of what Paul meant in Galatians 3:28 and how it was to be lived out in Pauline communities. In the Pauline communities, followers of Christ did not ignore or renounce their statuses; rather they were to live and to relate to one another as siblings as if there were no status differences. People were not to stop being women or men, and it did not change their status as Jew or non-Jew, slave or free, nor did it disengage them from the hierarchical structures of the Greco-Roman society. Instead, it redefined how people were to relate to one another within those statuses. Paul was not reinforcing the social structure in his statements but how to relate to one another in love, humility, and mutuality rather than in power and domination within those structures.

*Paul was not reinforcing the social structure but he redefined how people were to relate to one another within that structure.*

The uniqueness of the Pauline communities was not that its

members were living in liminality. Many communities experience this phenomenon. The unique aspect of the liminality of the in-Christ communities was that it did not eliminate the structures of society, but it redefined how people were to relate to one another within those structures. Christ transformed a highly stratified hierarchical community into one in which people served and loved one another like siblings. Power and privilege were gifts that were to be used for the empowerment and good of others.

*Chapter 8*

# The Prickly Passage

A book introducing a new narrative about women and men in the church would be incomplete without a discussion of 1 Timothy 2:11-15. We have called it the Prickly Passage because it is one of the most contested passages in the debate about gender roles in the church. There are many who use this text to support the exclusion of certain roles for women in the church. [191] However, throughout our discussion of the relationships of brothers and sisters in Christ, we have seen that Scripture promotes a mutuality and partnership of men and women in the church within their cultural context. An interpretation that excludes people from a particular role seems contradictory to the narrative about relationships that we have discussed so far. So we have to ask, "What was Paul trying to convey to the congregation at Ephesus, and how do we apply it in our churches today?"

Everyone brings a set of assumptions when interpreting this passage. We also bring a set of assumptions. Our set of assumptions are consistent with the relational narrative of this book. First, we believe that the narrative focus of Pauline writings is about the relationships between men and women. We approach the passage asking the question: "What was the behavior that Paul was correcting, and why did he correct it in the manner he did?" The second assumption we make is that there was a shared cultural context between Paul and the original readers which dictated appropriate public and domestic behavior in relationships. Third, Pauline letters were situational and were addressing questions or situations in a particular context. Therefore, there was shared information between Paul as the author and his readers that is implied in his letter. Another assumption we make is that Paul consistently in his letters addressed behavior of people that disrupted the life within the church or witness of the church to the broader society. So we ask, "How would the behavior disrupt the life of the church?"

The final assumption that we make is that the purpose of the instructions in 1 Timothy were missional. Paul was not only concerned about relationships within the church but also concerned about the character and witness of Christians to the broader society. The question we ask is, "How would this behavior affect the missional witness of the church?" This approach seems to be the most plausible explanation for Paul's writing and reconciles 1 Timothy 2:11-15 with other Pauline writings. In order to understand the passage, we must first understand the context in which the letter was written.

## Cultural Setting of Ephesus

Paul wrote his letter to Timothy, who was overseeing the church at Ephesus. During the first century, Ephesus was one of the major cities in the Roman Empire and was the Roman provincial capital of Asia. It had the third largest populace in the Roman Empire behind Rome and Athens.[192] It was a major seaport and was located at the crossroads of travel through the Roman Empire. As New Testament scholar Ada Spencer notes, "It was the way to Rome and the gateway to Asia with its harbor and connected to a major highway used by all who traveled west."[193]

Ephesus was a wealthy city. According to New Testament scholar Clinton Arnold, Ephesus was considered a leading city in one of the riches regions of the Roman Empire.[194] Commercially it was one of largest trading and shipbuilding centers in the Roman Empire, making it both a wealthy and multiethnic, cosmopolitan city.[195] It also had a flourishing tourist trade because of the temple of Artemis, which was considered one of the Seven Wonders of the World.[196] This wealth resulted in a reputation for luxury that was displayed not only in the temple but in individual households and by persons.[197]

Like other major Roman cities, Ephesus had a plethora of cults dedicated to the worship of gods and goddess. Clinton suggests that there were up to 50 different gods and goddesses that were worshipped in Ephesus.[198] The most dominant presence was Artemis.[199] There are several interpretations of who Artemis was and her function in the life of her followers. Scholars note that Artemis was believed by her followers to have authority over heaven and earth.[200] They also suggest her primary role was related to fertility. Keener more specifically states that her role was that of guardian of marriage and the family.[201] Many who followed Artemis believed that she could protect women though the dangers of childbearing. The deity was also believed to provide protection over the city of Ephesus and those who worshipped her.

The temple of Artemis also had an important economic function in the city as well. Keener notes that a significant portion of the city's wealth was connected with the temple.[202] It not only attracted a robust tourist trade, but it also acted as a bank for depositors. Additionally, funds from temple practices were used to sponsor various city projects such as building a gymnasium or other public buildings.[203]

Since some of the passages in Timothy are directed at the wealthy, it is useful to discuss the expectations of the wealthy to the Artemis cultic practices and to social life in general. Within religious practices, the wealthy competed for the honor and privilege of serving various functions in the temples. According to New Testament scholar Gary Hoag, wealthy leaders possessed considerable authority, and they expected to and served in distinguished roles in the temple. [204] Hoag notes, "Ephesus was the city of Artemis and the rich championed her fame."[205] They made offerings, competed for positions in the temple, funded her priesthood, performed her duties in her service, and trusted her with their wealth and safety."[206] In return, Artemis was believed to watch over their families, their riches and their future.[207]

The wealthy were expected to lead others in respecting, honoring, and serving the goddess Artemis.[208] They also expected distinguished positions within the city because of their status and competed regularly against peers for this distinction. The rich were expected to excel above others, both in appearance and appropriate social behavior. They received honor for appropriate gender-based appearance as noted by an "excellent external appearance compared to other younger men and women."[209] Conforming to appropriate social behavior meant demonstrating behavior expected of age and gender. For women this meant demonstrating modesty and silence in public.[210] According to Hoag, "Honor comes from honorable behavior."[211]

> *Conforming to appropriate social behavior meant demonstrating behavior expected of age and gender.*

Finally, we need to turn to the context of the Ephesian church itself. Acts 19 records that Paul's ministry quickly turned from the private synagogue meeting place to the public hall of Tyrannus. This hall was probably used for public lectures that were open to anyone. According to Keener, "Ephesus was a center for rhetoric in which public debate was normal."[212] He suggests that teaching in a public place Paul would have been recognized as a teacher of philosophy and attracted wealth patrons.[213] The church at Ephesus would have had people of a wide range of statuses.

We also know that the church was on public display. Paul's opponents complain that Paul had "led astray large number of people in Ephesus and in practically the whole province of Asia."[214] We also know from Acts 19 that the church was under scrutiny in a hostile environment. Romans in general were suspicious of new cults and religions, particularly those that undermined the traditional social order. In Ephesus not only was Christianity a new religion compared to the cult of Artemis, but it was disrupting the economics of the tourist trade and causing a public disturbance. Paul would have had these factors in mind when he wrote to Timothy in Ephesus. It is in this context that we now examine what Paul might have intended when he wrote 1 Timothy 2:11-15.

## The Textual Context of 1 Timothy 2:11-15

Just as it is important to understand the cultural context of a text, it is important to understand how passages fit into the overall purpose and argument of Paul's letter to Timothy. Paul's letters were situational; in other words, he is addressing specific questions, conflicts, or other problems that needed to be addressed in the church community. Therefore, we need to ask, "What was the purpose of this letter to Timothy?" Paul would have been concerned not only about the welfare of the church but also the witness of the church to the broader society. Conflict in the church not only harmed the unity of the church but also the witness of the church in a hostile environment. The question we ask approaching the passage is, "What kind of behavior was disrupting the relationships within the church and/or the witness of the church at Ephesus?"

There is a consensus among scholars that Paul's purpose in writing Timothy was to promote sound doctrine and to address false teaching that was threatening the life of the church at Ephesus.[215] Philip Towner suggests, "If there is one thing about these letters on which scholars do agree, it is that they purport to address church or mission situations in which false teachers or opponents figure quite prominently."[216] The nature of the false teaching is debated, but given the setting of the letter in Ephesus and the dominance of Artemis in the city, this is the most likely source of the false teaching.

> *Paul would have been concerned not only about the welfare of the church but also the witness of the church to the broader society.*

Next, we have to look at how our Prickly Passage fits into the purpose and structure of the letter as a whole. This helps to situate a passage in the logic of Paul's writing. Here we use the outline of 1 Timothy that Spencer uses in her commentary. Her outline makes clear Paul's purpose was to address false teaching so as to promote the missional life and witness of the church. Her outline is as follows:

1. *Paul reminds Timothy to warn the false teachers at Ephesus not to teach different doctrine (1:1-20).*

2. *In order that all may be saved and come to knowledge of the truth, Paul promotes peaceable prayer, education and leaders. (2:1-3:16)*

   *a. Paul urges living godly, peaceful lives (2:1-15).*

   *b. Godly leadership helps the church advance the truth (3:1-16)*

3. *Because God is savior of all, Timothy should teach the words of the faith, not heterodoxy, while making sure he sets an example of a faithful believer (4:1-5:2).*

4. *Church leaders should be honored and justly treated so that the church is not open to attack (5:3-6:2).*

5. *Timothy should fight his own fight of the faith, fleeing heterodox teaching (6:3-21).*[217]

The outline above emphasizes the relationship between false teaching and the mission of the church. Note that in Spencer's outline, our Prickly Passage fits into the section 1 Timothy 2:1-15 in which Paul is emphasizing the missional nature of the church. Paul is urging living peaceful lives so that all may be saved and come to the knowledge of Christ. In order to understand the Prickly Passage, we have to examine how Paul develops his narrative in 1 Timothy 2:1-15. We will consider these verses as the development of a single thought of living peaceable lives in order to further the gospel.

### *Exegesis of 1 Timothy 2:1-15*

One of the questions that needs to be answered as we study 1 Timothy 2:1-15 is who and what was Paul addressing and in what context. New Testament scholar Fred Long argues that a missional approach to 1 Timothy 2:1-15 suggests that Paul's instructions were not restricted to a worship context but were meant to address behavior in a broader social context. He states that Paul had "an acute concern for social respectability for the sake of effective witness."[218] He argues that the use of "all" in the passage indicates that there is a much broader scope of application of his instructions than just limited to worship activities.

The first part of the passage, 1 Timothy 2:1-7, provides the overall theme and emphasis of the passage. Long observes that 1 Timothy 2 starts with witness to the broadest level of society.[219] Believers are to make requests, prayers, and intercession for everyone, including kings and those in authority. They are to live quiet and peaceful lives in godliness and holiness. It is through these kinds of relationships that all people will come to a saving knowledge of Christ. This then is the focus of the passage. Men and women in Christ should live in such a way that their lives are a witness to the world. Paul then addresses groups of people more specifically in the verses that follow.

*Men and women in Christ should live in such a way that their lives are a witness to the world.*

In the next couple of verses, 1 Timothy 2:8-10, Paul then addresses how men and women specifically should live missionally.

The passage reads:

> 8 *I want men everywhere to lift up holy hands in prayer without anger or disputing.*
> 9 *I also want women to dress modestly, with decency and propriety, adorning themselves, not with elaborate hairstyles or gold or pearls or expensive clothes,*
> 10 *but with good deeds, appropriate for women who profess to worship God.*

The first instruction is to men in general. Men everywhere are to lift up holy hands in prayer without anger or disputing. Paul here corrects behaviors that were disruptive—anger and disputes. He urges them instead to behave in a way that indicates submission to God. Why would men be angry and disputing? One of the possible reasons was the competitiveness among people, particularly high-status men, for religious positions in their former worship of Artemis. However, the word "everywhere" also suggestions that this was not just practiced in a worship context but as a manner of life in witness to the broader society.[220] In a culture in which men would compete with others in rivalry, competition, and disputes, a missional witness was living in submission to God with quiet and godly lives. Not only did this promote harmonious relationships within the church, but this kind of life was recognized as virtuous in the broader Greco-Roman society.[221] Men were to be exemplary citizens in the community as witnesses for Christ.

The second command was addressed to women and is a parallel to the instruction for men. There are a number of reasons in the Ephesian context that women would wear braided hair and dress seductively. We are assuming that women in the church of Ephesus were doing this, because Paul admonishes them to stop doing it. One of the reasons women might have dressed like this is that women, like men, competed with one another for position and honor in the cult of Artemis and did so through dress. Women who could afford this luxury were in effect showing off their high status and competing with one another. Elsewhere in his letters, Paul confronts people for behavior that divides the church by status, particularly the wealthy.

Another possibility is that women in the church of Ephesus were following the fashion of "new Roman women," or as Long puts it, a kind of "feminist movement."[222] One of the characteristics of these new Roman women is that they wore clothing that was seductive.[223] Even modern Greco-Roman writers criticized women who followed this trend.[224] Women in the church who followed this trend would have not only brought criticism on their own behavior but also would have brought suspicion upon the church at Ephesus as promoting behavior that did not meet appropriate social norms.[225]

Both of these reasons are contextual possibilities for Paul's command to women in this verse. Their behavior was not just harmful to the church, but it also was considered a breach of appropriate social behavior. The Greco-Roman expectation of the well-bred, high status Roman woman was that she dress modestly and her riches be seen in good works.[226] In Paul's admonition he reinforced behavior for Christian women that would meet appropriate societal decorum for godly women so they would be exemplary witnesses to the broader society. They, like men, were to live quiet and peaceful lives in holiness and godliness as a witness to those around them.

In 2 Timothy 2:8-10 Paul is writing about behavior of Christians that was not limited to the disruption of relationships within the church but also harmful to the witness of the church to the broader society. Paul was aware that Christian behavior and actions were being scrutinized by both authorities and citizens around them. Throughout Paul's letters he reminds Christ followers that their lifestyles, conduct, and relationships were a missional witness to the broader society. As Long notes, "In other words, in 1 Timothy 2, Paul was merging prayer for missionary evangelism with a concern for social decorum and respectability as reflected elsewhere in the Pauline corpus. For us, a better heading (if we need one) for 1 Timothy 2:1-15 would be 'Prayer and Instructions for Missional Living.' "[227]

Now we turn to our Prickly Passage, 1 Timothy 2:11-15. New Testament scholar Philip Payne notes, "The only verse in the Bible alleged to explicitly prohibit women from teaching or having authority over men is 1 Timothy 2:12."[228] However, this verse cannot stand alone but must be read in context. There are a number of exegetical issues within this passage, so we consider each of these in turn. Two questions are at the heart of the controversy concerning this passage: 1. "What behavior was Paul not permitting and why?" 2. "Is the behavior situational or universal?" We examine both of these questions within the context of Paul's concern for the missional witness of the church, which is the emphasis of this passage's context. Our Prickly Passage reads as follows:

> 11 A woman should learn in quietness and full submission.
> 12 I do not permit a woman to teach or assume authority over a man; she must be quiet
> 13 For Adam was formed first, then Eve.
> 14 And Adam was not the one deceived; it was the woman who was deceived and became a sinner.
> 15 But women will be saved through childbearing–if they continue in faith, love and holiness with propriety.[229]

The first questions that need to be addressed in interpreting the 1 Timothy 2 passage are who, where, and what was Paul addressing.

In verses 1-15, Paul starts with the plural women and men and then in following verses changes to the singular man and woman. Scholars have suggested that the switch in wording signals that Paul is switching from addressing men and women in general to husband and wife specifically.[230] The reason for this conclusion is that Paul's discussion of living missionally within the Greco-Roman society in 1 Timothy 2:1-15 progresses from living missionally first as citizens, then as men and women generally, and finally as husband and wives.

The household was the cornerstone of Greco-Roman society, and it was important that the relationship between husbands and wives was a missional witness to the broader society so that the church at Ephesus would not be discredited. As Long explains, "Such scrutiny was especially directed to religious activities of various kinds; a new religious group like the early Christ-followers was not exempt from scrutiny from these mores, but, if anything was more vulnerable to social stigmatization, if not even suspicion of political subversion. Traditionally, the Romans were suspicious of new cults and their satirists and moralists (like Plutarch and Juvenal) blamed the gullibility of women for the spread of such cults."[231] Just as in the previous chapter's discussion about the marriage relationship in Ephesians, Paul is not reinforcing structure but emphasizing how to live out the new mutual relationships as brothers and sisters in Christ in the context of marriage in a way that attracts people to Christ. We will discuss each of the verses in turn.

*it was important that the relationship between husbands and wives was a missional witness to the broader society*

Paul's first command, "A woman should learn in quietness and full submission," expresses the cultural expectations of a wife in public in Greco-Roman society. According to Long, "Quietness too was a social virtue of wives in public in relation to their husbands."[232] Long notes that although Roman women were given greater freedom in participation in public venues outside the home, social critics still denounced women speaking in public gatherings.[233] Long also comments that the emphasis of Paul's command was for a wife to learn, which is something that was highly valued in the Pauline churches.[234] Wives were to be full, mutual participants in the spiritual life of the household.

The next verse needs to be discussed in detail: "I do not permit a woman to teach or to assume authority over a man; she must be quiet." Although this has been used to restrict women's roles in the church, we would like to point out that Paul is speaking about actions not roles. The verse reads that Paul does not permit a woman to teach, which is an action but does not refer to a role, that of teacher. It is a subtle but important distinction. Instead of asking what role Paul was not permitting, the question we need to ask is: "What actions was he not permitting in this context and why?"

There are many exegetical issues with this single verse that result in different interpretive outcomes, so we will take each in turn. The first choice is the Greek word ἐπιτρέπω, epitrepó, which is translated "permit." Paul writes, "I do not permit." The question that this raises is whether Paul used this phrase to command a universal, permanent application of what follows or is giving advice for a particular situation. Payne does an extensive study on the use of ἐπιτρέπω and found that

> "What actions was he not permitting in this context and why?"

its use in the Old Testament is always referring to a specific situation, not a universal command. He also finds that in most cases in the New

Testament it also refers to a specific situation or is given for a limited duration.[235] If, as Payne suggests, the prohibition is temporally and situationally limited, we need to ask what Paul was limiting and why.

The prohibition contains two verbs, teach and to assume authority. The Greek construction joins these two verbs into a single thought.[236] The verb translated "teach" is rather straightforward in the Greek as it is in the English. Generally it is used as in English to convey the action of imparting knowledge or skills to another person. This is how it is most frequently used by Paul in his other writings as well.[237] Teaching has a positive connotation, and in many places Paul talks about women who teach. In the list of gifts, as with other gifts, teaching is gender neutral.

However, teaching is paired with authority. One difficulty in interpreting this passage is the word αὐθεντέω, or authenteó, that is translated as "authority." This word is only used once in the New Testament and is not the usual word Paul uses when he discusses authority in the church. There are two different thoughts on how this word was used in the broader Greek literature. It is sometimes used in a positive way, as it is translated above. But more frequently it is used in a negative way, referring to some kind of destructive behavior against another's will. Johann Louw and Eugene Nida translate the word as "control." Westfall describes it as follows:

> In the Greek corpus, the verb αὐθεντέω refers to a range of actions that are not restricted to murder or violence. However, the people who are the targets of these actions are harmed, forced against their will (compelled), or at least their self-interests are overridden, because the actions involve the imposition of the subject's will over against the recipient's will, ranging from dishonor to lethal action.[238]

Bible translations that have this sense of the word translate it as usurp, domineer, control, initiate violence, etc.[239] One possible interpretation is to render the translation "a wife to teach with domineering authority over her husband." In Paul's context it would be unacceptable for a wife to publically teach a husband and even more so in a domineering way.

*Husbands and wives were to follow social decorum in order to be a missional witness to the broader society.*

As Long notes, "Instead of teaching or domineering a husband (both unacceptable behaviors in Greco-Roman context) the wife was to remain quiet; it was not her 'station' to teach her husband."[240] The two verses provide parallel contrasts between learn in silence and teach, and submission and domineering, reinforcing the proposal that Paul was referring to the behavior of wives in this context. Wives in this context were behaving in such a way that could bring scrutiny and criticism to the church. Husbands and wives were to follow social decorum in order to be a missional witness to the broader society.[241] The use of the word "permit" also makes it unlikely that it was meant to be a universal or permanent prohibition.[242] Paul was addressing a particular socio-cultural context so that husbands and wives, by their behavior, were a missional witness within that context.

The citation of the Genesis account has often been used as evidence that Paul had intended that the prohibition was meant to be universal, for all people for all time. There are several possibilities for the analogy that Paul was making by citing the Genesis account. One possibility is that he was making an analogous comparison to being deceived by false teaching. Wives were deceived by false beliefs and teaching them to their husbands, just as Eve was deceived by the serpent and led Adam astray by false teaching. Therefore, a wife should learn first. The second possible comparison is to refute false teachings based on the mythology of the Artemis cult that woman was the originator of man, and it was the man who had been deceived.[243] A third possibility is that the emergence of the Roman "new woman" led to wives usurping the public roles of their husbands."[244] If this was the situation, then Paul was using the Genesis account to demonstrate the mutuality of the relationships between men and women in creation.[245] As Payne notes, "For women to assume authority for themselves over men disrespects men."[246] Any of these comparisons are plausible in this context.

The final statement in our Prickly Passage is about safety in childbearing. We have to remember that Paul is writing in a context where people believed that spirits caused illness and harm. Women prayed to Artemis believing that she could protect them in childbirth. It is somewhat difficult for Westerners to imagine a world filled with spirits that would cause harm. But as I (Sue) was working in a church on the other side of the world, one of the questions people asked about Christianity was, "If I burn all my magic paraphernalia, who is going to protect me from the spirits?" It required a lot of trust for new converts to trust solely in Christ rather than the protection they sought from magic. It would be similar for the women in Ephesus. For centuries they had prayed to Artemis for protection, and now they were being asked to choose, to serve God or to serve Artemis, to trust God or trust Artemis. For them it was a very real choice. Hoag states, "Women who chose to serve God rather than the goddess for childbearing would put their lives at risk because of the possibility of the wrath of the goddess."[247] Paul, however, assures them that God will protect them in childbearing.

## *Conclusion: What Does it Mean for Us*

Placing 1 Timothy 2:11-15 in both its cultural and its literary context highlights Paul's emphasis on living in a culturally appropriate way in order to be a witness in the broader social context. This involved behaving in ways that were not disruptive to the social relationships in the church as well as living appropriate lives in the world. Many times in Scripture, Paul instructs people that they have freedom in Christ, but for the sake of the witness of the church they are to refrain from acting on that freedom. For instance, they have freedom to eat meat offered to idols, but if it is going to harm their brother or sister, they should refrain. If it will send mixed signals to their neighbors, they should refrain. He also writes elsewhere of maintaining appropriate social decorum in social relationships. Later in the same letter he instructs Timothy, "Do not rebuke an older man harshly but exhort him as if he were your father."[248] In Timothy's context, it would be inappropriate and disrespectful for a younger person to correct an elder.

The question we need to ask ourselves is how should we live so that our lives are a witness for Christ? The ancient apologists knew how important it was for Christians to be exemplary citizens. Today it is vitally important in a world that is increasingly hostile to Christianity that our lives and relationships are a missional witness. Our behavior is a witness, but sometimes it is not missional. I remember sitting with several pastors in a closed country during the era when a number of well-known American pastors had highly visible moral failings. The pastors turned to me and said, "What is it with you Americans? Don't you know how hard it is to witness in this country when all that the public media shows is how immoral Christians are!" But we don't have to go overseas to see how our relationships and behavior affect our witness. Ask servers in restaurants how they feel about working on

Sunday. Many hate it because it is when the "church crowd" comes in, and they are known for being stingy. Ouch!

As we become more globally connected and have more communication with our global brothers and sisters, we need to recognize there are different standards for appropriate behavior for people, especially between men and women. I (Sue) remember driving out to my village with my fiancé and reminding him, "Don't touch me." Any public contact between men and women was inappropriate in that culture. Imagine what non-Christians in the community would think about some of the behavior of visiting Western men and women. Sometimes I was asked concerning visiting ministry teams, "Are they Christian?"

Let me (Sue) tell one more story about respecting social decorum in relationships as a witness for Christ. In the small language group in which I worked, young people, both men and women, were under the authority of the elders. Young pastors who had Bible training were expected to respect the authority of the church elders no matter how well trained they were. I know of one case in which a pastor was asked to leave when he tried to usurp the authority of the elders. This also meant that younger people could not correct elders or preach to them.

I never understood the impact of this until we were completing the translation of the New Testament and still needed to check the translation with non-Christians. When the translation committee chairman asked me to explain what that translation check was, I told him it was when we read Scripture to people who weren't part of the translation process to make sure they understood it. He looked at me and said, "What a great way to do evangelism. We can't preach to older people but we can ask for their help. We can go up to them and ask them if it is well-written Galat."

A few weeks later I returned to the village to find two young men and the chairman of the translation committee waiting for me. The chairman explained to me that these two young men were going to be the readers. They had chosen 14 villages that were hostile to the gospel to check the translation. For two years they went to one of these villages every day and sat and read to the village. They respectfully asked the villagers if they understood the meaning of the text and if the language was clear and appropriate. After two years the chairman of the translation committee said, "Okay, they are ready." On Christmas Day, 300 people were baptized, and churches were planted in seven villages. Because they respected and followed the social decorum for relationships between young and old in Galat culture, these young evangelists were able to be a missional witness to these communities.

*Paul consistently applied the principle of promoting sibling-like relationships within their cultural context so in-Christ communities would be a missional witness to the society in which they lived.*

Paul's heart was for reaching every person for Jesus Christ. Paul consistently applied the principle of promoting sibling-like relationships within their cultural context so the in-Christ communities would be a missional witness to the society in which they lived. Interpreting these verses as a prohibition of certain roles for women (or men) is antithetical to the inclusion of women in Jesus' ministry as well as Paul's teaching about the mutual relationships of the in-Christ community. How Paul specifically applies these principles can only be understood in the specific context for which he writes them.

Paul's message to us today is that we are to live transformed lives within our cultural context. And through living in a new way as brothers and sisters in Christ within our cultural context, we are to be missional witnesses to the power of Christ. It is true; they will know us by our love for one another as we respect each other and those around us. Paul was not only concerned for the relationships within the church but also that the love we have for one another as brothers and sisters in Christ would reflect Christ to the world.

*Chapter 9*

# Conclusion

Well, here we are. We have taken a journey from those first relationships in the Garden, through their fall, and back to their redemption through Christ. We have made the case that the narrative focus of the New Testament concerning men and women is relationship. Jesus came to restore the relationship between men and women that we were created to have—partners together serving God, each other, and creation.

What started in the Garden was marred by the fall. Our relationships became broken, not only broken, but sin became embedded into our society. Created as image bearers we became categories based on our statuses: men, women, Jew, Gentile, free, slave. These categories became a barrier, and rather than a partnership of persons, we, men and women, became "us" and "them."

But Jesus came to redeem our relationships. He showed us how it could be done. Status didn't matter in His kingdom. People were "in" or "out" based on only one thing—responding to him. We were once again brothers and sisters in a new family, his family. Partners in ministry!

The story continues in Acts where the Spirit created a new community, a community in Christ in which there was no distinction in status in the community between men and women, slave and free, or Jew and Gentile. All were included; all were given the same Spirit. The Spirit did not erase these social distinctions, but rather people could live out this new kind of sibling-like relationship within their social statuses.

In Paul's world this meant living out sibling-like relationships within a highly stratified society. Paul's instructions, when consistently read, instruct people how to live their new brother-and-sister relationship within these statuses and roles rather than reinforcing or establishing the social arrangements of roles. Paul is teaching a new way of relating, not prescribing particular gender roles for all people and all times. He was teaching how to live out these new liminal relationships within the structures of his society, a very hierarchical, patriarchal society where honor and shame reinforced hierarchy and power. He did this because he not only wanted people to have harmonious relationships within the church, but he also wanted the way that they lived to be a missional witness to the society around them.

> *Paul is teaching a new way of relating, not prescribing particular gender roles for all people and all times.*

We continue to live in-between the times, the already-not yet. We have a new identity and through the Spirit can live in redeemed relationships as brothers and sisters in Christ. However, because we are between the times, we must live out these sibling-like relationships within the structures of our societies in a way that is a missional witness. This means that people in every culture will need to determine what this looks like for their church. Even within specific cultures, different churches—Anglican, Baptist, Pentecostal—will express this sibling-like relationship in various formations and structural arrangement of roles. However, there are some basic principles of how sibling-like relationships can be lived out in social statuses in different cultures.

## Using Privilege to Empower Others

The first principle of sibling-like relationships is that those who have statuses of privilege and power are to use them to include and empower others, not to exclude and dominate others. Some cultures have a more hierarchical arrangement of roles and others a more egalitarian, but every culture has statuses that allow more access to resources, positions, and wealth. People in the early church were not the same. They had different amounts of wealth; there were different ethnicities, genders, occupations, etc. Likewise, people in the in-Christ community today are not the same. All of us have privilege in certain contexts. I (Sue) am a white, middle-class, educated woman. As such I have access to opportunities and resources that others don't. I need to look for ways in which I can use my access to resources to help others. For instance, I can work with younger scholars to enable them to participate in conferences or publish articles. In the same way, those with privilege can provide opportunities for those who are on the margins of our communities so they can have a voice in decision-making.

Since we all have privilege in some contexts, rather than be embarrassed by it, we need to acknowledge the good gifts that God has given us and use them to empower our brothers and sisters in Christ. We are also to extend that same kind of inclusion and service to those outside the in-Christ community. We need to ask if there are ways in which we can use our opportunities and gifts to serve others. It may be as simple as being generous when we hire someone to do odd jobs or tipping well when we eat out. It may be a church helping with immigration documentation or offering English lessons for those who have just arrived in our communities.

This also means that we do not sit back when someone or a group of people use their privilege to harm, dominate, dehumanize, or exclude others. No! This is when those with privilege and power must use it to help those who cannot help themselves. Much like the lame man at the Beautiful Gate (Acts 3:2), there are always those who are born into unfortunate circumstances beyond their control. One cannot read newspaper headlines without hearing the stories of people who are refugees, are homeless, in poverty, in modern slavery, suffering from AIDS, in the grips of addiction. In Genesis 1 and 2 we learned that God's image bearers are called to care, create, and cultivate in ways so that all of God's creation flourishes. In order to do that, those who have power and privilege must work to hear the voices of others. Professor, pastor, and author Ken Wytsma reminds us, "Everyone has a voice, and we don't need to speak for them. Instead we need to understand and address the processes that steal their voices or the

*we need to acknowledge the good gifts that God has given us and use them to empower our brothers and sisters in Christ.*

reasons we aren't hearing from them."[249] We listen to those without power and privilege, and we act, using our power and privilege to ennoble others, so that they too can flourish. Simply put, we are to "do justice, and to love kindness, and to walk humbly with our God."[250]

### Sharing Our Gifts

A second principle of living sibling-like relationships in structure is that we need to consider our resources and gifts as belonging to each other. This past spring our ministry (Jackie) invited Sue to come and speak on siblinghood. She shared with us what's been mentioned previously in this book—that her doctorate

*God's image bearers are called to care, create, and cultivate in ways so all of God's creation flourishes.*

was viewed as the "community's doctorate." She went on to make her point, asking who in the room had doctorates (academic or medical). There were eleven doctorates in all. Sue stated, "We, collectively in this room, have eleven doctorates." They are not Jackie's or Rene's or Pete's, they are "ours." After that weekend, one of the attendees went back to her organization and accumulated all the resources they had collectively on their staff—the hours of a particular skill, the number of educational degrees, years of experience, etc. She then shared with her staff, "The next time you have a problem you can't solve, realize these are the resources we collectively have in our office and at your disposal." This would be a creative way for our churches to view the congregation and resources available to a particular church community. Imagine the ministries that might bubble up from the collective resources already present in the body of Christ.

We can rejoice in the gifts God has given us because we can share them with others. Each of us was created with different gifts and talents. We (Jackie and Sue) are very different and have different personalities and gifting. It took both of us to write this book. God gave us different gifts to use for the building up of each other and the body of Christ. Can you imagine if we spent time on Sunday morning visually acknowledging the gifts and ministries of people in the church? Every fall we could call up everyone involved in education and lay hands and pray for them as we commission them for the ministry to which God had called them. On another day, we could call up everyone who works in healthcare and do the same thing, and then at a different time people in food preparation or retail or service industries. You get the picture. It would radically change how we understand the ministries of our church.

*We can rejoice in the gifts God has given us because we can share them with others.*

We don't have to envy or desire a gift that someone else possesses, because as a family it belongs to all of us. We can appreciate the gifts that God has given to someone else and be joyful in being able to contribute ours to the family. I (Sue) appreciate Jackie's ability to preach. Just after Easter, a teammate on my triathlon team asked me if I was tired after the weekend. He assumed because I taught at a seminary that I also was a pastor. I assured him that I was quite comfortable in my ivory tower and appreciated those who had the gifting and calling to be a pastor. Jackie's schedule would kill me!

*Humility is recognizing the gifts we have been given are to serve others.*

As brothers and sisters we can rejoice and admire those who God has gifted to serve the church in ways that we are not gifted. We can also rejoice in the gifts that God has given us to serve our brothers and sisters. Humility is not hiding our gifts or pretending we don't have them. Humility is recognizing the gifts we have been given are to serve others.

## Respecting Other People

A third principle of living sibling-like relationships in structure is that we need to be cautious about making statements about people and roles based on statuses. When we categorize a certain group of people as having a particular characteristic, we dehumanize individuals. It is much easier to dismiss or degrade others when we turn them into the "other" by categorizing people based on status. We are no longer Sue or Jackie, but rather women. We can even problematize people who don't know Jesus as "the unsaved." The story of redemption is a story about the redemption of relationships, between persons, about individuals whom God created. We need to talk about specific people rather than categories based on status. If we can't say, "Sue shouldn't teach because she was deceived or she lacks education," then we shouldn't say that about a class based on status, "Women shouldn't teach because they were deceived, or they lack education." The same goes for the people who are poor, immigrants, homeless, etc.

Perhaps we need to reevaluate the church's teaching on these groups in light of this new lens being presented. We need to reevaluate decisions that are made from our assumptions of people in one of these categories. We need to remind ourselves that people aren't categories, but rather they are individuals. We need to be willing to listen to people who are unlike ourselves in order to understand their viewpoint, their history, their life. As leaders, we need to provide opportunities to hear the voices with stories different than our own. We need to be willing to listen to how they have experienced life, what their fears are, how policies have affected them, what their desires are. We need each other to widen our perspectives and provide a greater understanding of the world and the church. It is in relationships that we can work together to bridge divides between "us" and "them."

We also need to accept how people in other cultures and other churches work out these principles in their context. Living as brothers and sisters in Christ will look very different for the church in Asia, in Latin America, or in Africa than for a church in North America. Roles assigned to statuses and the arrangement and expectations of those roles vary from culture to culture. We should not try to impose our cultural ideas about roles and role relationships. Churches in different cultures must work out how to live sibling-like relationships within their own structures. However, we can learn much from each other, because we are brothers and sisters in Christ.

> *Living as brothers and sisters in Christ will look very different for the church in Asia, in Latin America, or in Africa than for a church in North America.*

## Not Fearing Sexuality

While reading this book, one of my (Sue) students asked us to address the romantic-narrative in the church, especially in the context of the revelations of sexual abuse and sexual misconduct in the church.

As a member of a church staff working with young adults, she resonated with Jackie's story about the fear of one her classmates to give her a ride because she was a woman.

We need to replace the romantic-danger narrative that has influenced the conversations about men and women in the church with the narrative of brother-sister relationships. The sibling-like relationships are just that, sibling-like, a deep loving relationship. They are not sexual; they are relational. We can love one another without sexual intent: men and women, men and men, women and women. In our oversexed culture, thinking of each other as brothers and sisters provides a way of being able to relate to one another in a safe way. The sibling narrative provides another way of talking about relationships within youth groups, within adult groups, etc.

We especially need this narrative not only in our horizontal relationships but also when power is involved. Those of us in leadership are responsible for providing a safe environment in which people can flourish without worrying about sexual advances. Most corporations are required to provide sexual harassment training; but how would our behavior change if we first ask, "How would I feel about this being said to my sister, my daughter, my son, my brother?" As Christians, we need to have higher standards. We are not even to think of one another as potential sexual partners but as brothers and sisters in Christ.

*In our oversexed culture, thinking of each other as brothers and sisters provides a way of being able to relate to one another in a safe way.*

Let me (Sue) give an example. As anthropologists we study incest rules. These are rules regarding those people with whom you cannot marry or have sexual relations. These vary greatly across cultures. In the language group in which I worked, a person could not marry anyone they were related to, extending to fourth or fifth cousins. In other cultures, like North American, this only extends to first cousin.

*We should not have to worry about sexual harassment or sexual misconduct, because as brothers and sisters, these kinds of actions are not even part of our thought process.*

Anthropologists have many explanations about why these rules exist, but none really explain all the variations. One day I decided to map all prohibitions on sexual relations found in Leviticus on a genealogy chart. I found that the prohibited sexual relations were between men and women who needed to live and work together on a regular basis. The common theme of incest rules was that they provided safe relationships between men and women who lived and worked together. They created a safe environment for men and women to flourish in which they did not have to worry about sexual advances.

Teaching about brother-and-sister relationships changes the way we see each other. Our North American culture tends to promote seeing everyone as a potential sexual partner. However, in the church, we need to create an environment in which men and women can relate and work together in a safe environment. We should not have to worry about sexual harassment or sexual misconduct, because as brothers and sisters, these kinds of actions are not even part of our thought process. Rather than focusing on the wrong kind of relationships, we need to teach about the right kind of relationships. An excellent book that goes more in-depth in this discussion is *Mixed Ministry: Working Together as Brothers and Sisters in an Oversexed Society.*[251]

## Final Thoughts

There is a lot more that could be said about living out our relations as brothers and sisters in Christ. How we live out this new kind of relationship within our structures will look differently in different cultures, different church traditions, and even different families. There is a lot more that needs to be written about what this looks like, but that will have to wait for another book. However, what we do know is that as the early Christians lived this new kind of relationship in the social structures in which they lived, they transformed the world.

We may have to agree to disagree with each other about roles and arrangement of roles between men and women in the church and home, but I think we can agree on the type of relationships we

> *Rather than be in two camps, egalitarian or complementarian, we can be in one camp, that of brothers and sisters in Christ.*

are to have with one another. We believe that by emphasizing the sibling-like relationship between men and women we will find that there is a lot more that unites us than divides us. Rather than be in two camps, egalitarian or complementarian, we can be in one camp, that of brothers and sisters in Christ. It is this unity and love that we have for one another that will win the world for Jesus Christ!

# Acknowledgments

Books are not written in isolation but require the collaboration, encouragement and enthusiasm of friends and colleagues, who gently critique, make suggestions and most of all believe in the author. This book has been the product of many conversations over several years. We so are grateful that our unique journeys brought us together to write this book.

### Sue

I want to thank Dr. S. Scott Bartchy who was my Ph.D. supervisor at UCLA. I had the privilege of sitting in his classes on early Christianity in which he emphasized the "lived out" experience of the early Christ-followers. In his contrast between the values and the behaviors of Greco-Roman society and the early Christian communities I recognized their similarity to Victor Turner's theoretical framework of structure and antistructure that we use in this book.

I am thankful the opportunities to present these ideas in their rough form at the Evangelical Theological Society. The questions and comments from colleagues were important for refining these ideas. One particular question from the late Dr. Robert Saucy was the impetus for formulating the foundational ideas about the social dimension of inaugurated eschatology.

I am thankful to the men and women at the Marcella Summits who heard these ideas and provided feedback and encouragement. I particularly want to thank several who read very rough copies of this book and gave suggestions on how to make it better. The chapter on Prickly Passages was written at their request.

I want to thank the men and women in my Women and Missions class who read a draft of this book. Their thoughtful critique and suggestions from many perspectives are reflected in this book. I am also thankful for the PhD students at Asbury Theological Seminary who provided much needed cross-cultural perspective.

I also am grateful to the many people who have expressed their enthusiasm for this project. These conversations are too numerous to count, but I want to thank each person who listened carefully as I articulated these ideas and encouraged me that this book was a much needed conversation.

I am extremely grateful to Nancy Hoffman who has read this draft numerous times. She sat for a week with Jackie and me as we read through this book recording our comments. She proofed this book several times, and each time made it a better product.

I am especially thankful to Jackie Roese who"hunted me down." These ideas had been relegated to the back burner during the contingency of the immediate. She saw something important and worthwhile in them and asked me to present them at her Marcella Summit. It was at the first Marcella Summit that this book began to take shape. She encouraged me to communicate in a way that is engaging and accessible. Her enthusiasm, humor, patience, and camaraderie kept this book alive.

## *Jackie*

Sue has done a marvelous job of acknowledging many who deserve credit for the ideas conveyed in this book.

My journey in formulating these ideas has been like putting a puzzle together. First and foremost I must acknowledge the courage of the leadership at Irving Bible Church. They gave me the freedom to pursue, research and question the roles of men and women.

From there I must credit the plethora of authors who gave their time, study and skill to writing books that helped me learn what I couldn't learn otherwise. I was able to grab different pieces of the puzzle from them.

Alongside authors, I too want to acknowledge those men and women who had numerous conversations that helped shaped my thinking. Dr. Sarah Sumner, Dr. Scot McKnight, Dr. Philip Payne, Dr. Lauren Winner, Dr. Halee Gray Scott and Carolyn Custis James—to name a few.

And I want to thank Dr. Sue Russell for thinking outside the box. It was her unique skill set and expertise that helped fill in the puzzle. Upon hearing her present at ETS (Evangelical Theological Society) I immediately knew her ideas could be instrumental in working through the impasse the Church faces about the role of men and women. Ideas are built upon other ideas and ideas birth movements.

## *And from both of us*

We are also grateful for you, our reader, who has joined us in this conversation. If we were able, we would love to sit down with each one of you and hear your stories. It is conversations like these that have enriched our lives and made this book possible.

Most of all, we are grateful to a gracious Lord and God, who has gifted us, inspired us, and created us in a community in which we can learn, encourage, and share. It is our hope, that this book reflects the good gifts that He has given us.

# End Notes

## *Chapter 1: A New Conversation*

1   A good resource that outlines the two views and provides a discussion of the strengths and weaknesses of both is James R. Beck ed., *Two Views on Women in Ministry* (Grand Rapids, MI: Zondervan, 2005).

## *Chapter 2: Partners in Paradise*

2   Genesis 1:1-31.

3   For further insight, refer to Dorothy Sayer's book, *Are Women Human?* (Grand Rapids, MI: Eerdmans, 1971).

4   Christopher J.H. Wright, *Deuteronomy* (Peabody, MA: Hendrickson Publishers, Inc., 1996), 11.

5   http://www.theopedia.com/Perichoresis

6   Stephen Boyd, *The Men We Long To Be* (Eugene, OR: Wipf and Stock Publishers, 1997), 118.

7   Carolyn Custis James, *Half the Church* (Grand Rapids, MI: Zondervan, 2010), 56.

8   Phyllis Trible in her book *God and the Rhetoric of Sexuality* (Philadelphia: Fortress Press, 1973) explains that " 'To till and to keep' connotes not plunder and rape but care and attention...work changes human life from passivity to participation," 85.

9   The forbidden tree spells the limitations to human dominion. Trible, *God and Rhetoric*, 78.

10  Scot McKnight explains, "Adam and Eve are God's appointed ruling image-bearers (Gen 1:26-27). What are image-bearers to do? They are appointed to rule for God, or under God. The 'fall' is from this task. That is, Adam and Eve decide they want to rule 'like God' instead of ruling 'under God,' which means Adam and Eve are usurpers....The story of sin in the Bible is the story of God's elect people wanting to be God-like instead of godly, of ruling instead of sub-ruling and being ruled." Scot McKnight, *Kingdom Conspiracy* (Grand Rapids, MI: Brazos Press, 2014), 28-29.

11  Man (*ha-adam*) called woman *'ishah* (woman), having been taken from *'ish* (man). These are the customary words in Hebrew to differentiate man and woman; neither term is a personal name. Adam names the woman "Eve" after the fall. (Genesis 3:20)

12  Reference Brené Brown's book *Daring Greatly* (New York: Penguin Group, 2014) and Matthew D. Lieberman's book *Social: Why Our Brains Are Wired to Connect* (New York: Crown Publishers, 2013).

13  Lieberman, *Social,* 64.

14  This is not unique to mankind. In Genesis 1:22, God used similar language in reference to the sea creatures and birds. "And God blessed them, saying, 'Be fruitful and multiply and fill the waters in the seas, and let birds multiply on the earth.'"

15  Translation and italics our own.

16  http://www.patheos.com/blogs/jesuscreed/2014/05/22/all-humanity-is-the-image-of-god-rjs/

17  Carolyn Custis James, *Malestrom* (Grand Rapids, MI: Zondervan, 2015), 51.

18  Bernd Wannenwetsch, Classnotes from "The Moral Fit: A Fresh Look at the Relationship of the Sexes," Regent College, July 11-22, 2011.

19  Matthew 22:30.

20  "The two are one flesh" is a Hebrew expression meaning they form a single being.

21  Brown, *Daring Greatly,* 34.

22  Brown, *Daring Greatly,* 39.

### *Chapter 3: Relationships in Ruin*

23  Genesis 3:16b.

24  Paul Barnett, *The Rise of Early Christianity* (Downers Grove, IL: InterVarsity Press, 1999).

25  Everett Ferguson, *Backgrounds of Early Christianity* (Grand Rapids, MI: Eerdmans, 2003), 14.

26  Ibid., 150.

27  Loren and David J. Hamilton with Janice Rogers Cunningham, *Why Not Women* (Seattle: YWAM, 2000), 72.

28  Homer, *Iliad, Volume I: Books 1-12*, trans. A.T. Murray (Cambridge: Harvard University Press, 1924), 8:161-166.

29  Homer, *Iliad, Volume II: Books 13-24*, trans. A. T. Murray (Cambridge: Harvard University Press, 1925), 15:10-16.

30  Hesiod, "Theogony" in *The Homeric Hymns and Momerica*, trans. Hugh G. Evelyn-White (Cambridge: Harvard University Press, 1954), 85.

31  Ibid., 590-605.

32  Ibid., 610.

33  Hesiod, *Works and Days*, trans. M. L. West (Oxford: Clarendon Press, 1996), 380.

34  Ibid., 406.

35  Aristotle, *Politics*, trans. H. Rackham (Cambridge: Harvard University Press, 1950), 1254b:12.

36  Aristotle, "Generation of Animals," in *The Complete Works of Aristotle*, ed. Jonathon Barnes (Princeton: Princeton University Press, 1984), 731:25-25. In the generation of a new life, he also states that it is the man who provides the soul and the female who contributes the matter.

37  Ibid., 732:5-10.

38  Ibid., 767:25-32.

39  Aristotle, "Physiognomics," in *The Complete Works of Aristotle*, ed. Jonathon Barnes (Princeton: Princeton University Press, 1984), 809b: 5-10.

40  Aristotle, "History of Animals," in *The Complete Works of Aristotle*, ed. Jonathon Barnes (Princeton: Princeton University Press, 1984), 608b: 5-15.

41  Plato, *The Republic, Vol. I*, trans. Paul Shorey (Cambridge: Harvard University Press, 1946), 447.

42  Plato, *Law, Vol. I*, trans. R. G. Bury (Cambridge: Harvard University Press, 1952), 448.

43  Philo, *The Works of Philo*, trans. C. D. Yonge (Peabody, MA: Hendrickson Publishers, 1993), 21.

44  Ibid., 796.

45  Ibid., 796.

46  Ibid., 798.

47  Ibid., 23.

48  Ibid., 23.

49  Ibid., 23.

50  Judith Baskin, *Misdrashic Women: Formations in the Feminine in Rabbinic Literature* (London: Brandeis University Press, 2002), 3.

51  Judith Romney Wegner, *Chattel or Person?: The Status of Women in the Mishnah* (Oxford: Oxford University Press, 1988), 4.

52  Ronald W. Pierce, "From Old Testament Law to New Testament Gospel" in *Discovering Biblical Equality: Complementarity Without Hierarchy*, eds. Ronald W. Pierce and Rebecca Merrill Groothuis (Downers Grove, IL: IVP Academic, 2005), 107.

53  Ibid., 105.

54  Wegner, *Chattel or Person*, 6.

55  Ibid., 18.

56  Theodore Friedman, "The Shifting Role of Women, From the Bible to Talmud" in *Judaism* (Fall 1987), Vol. 36, Issue 4481.

57  Karen J. Torjesen, *When Women Were Priests: Women's Leadership in the Early Church and the Scandal of Their Subordination in the Rise of Christianity* (San Francisco: HarperSanFrancisco, 1995).

58  Freidman, "Shifting Role," 481.

59  Bereshth Rabbah 18.1, as quoted in Freidman, 481.

60  Wegner, *Chattel or Person*, 19.

61   *The Mishnah*. m. Qid 1:7.

62   Wegner, *Chattel or Person*, 146.

63   *Mishnah*, m. Sortah 3:4.

64   Ibid., m. Shab 2:6.

65   Wegner, *Chattel or Person*, 156.

66   Loren Cunningham, David J. Hamilton, and Janice Rogers, *Why Not Women* (Seattle: YWAM, 2000), 72-103.

67   Wegner, *Chattel or Person*, 163.

68   Ibid., 166.

69   tBer 7:18 quoted from Tal Ilan, *Jewish Women in Greco-Roman Palestine* (Peabody: Hendrickson Publishers, Inc., 1996), 176.

70   Meyer Reinhold, "Usurption of Status and Status Symbols in the Roman Empire" in *Historia: Zeitschrift für alte Geschichte* 20:3 (1971), 275-302.

71   Peter Garnsey and Richard Saller, *The Roman Empire: Economy, Society, and Culture* (Berkley: University of California Press, 1987), 118-123.

72   Jon E. Lendon, *Empire of Honour* (Oxford: Oxford University Press, 1997), 37.

73   Garnsey and Saller, *The Roman Empire*, 121.

74   Lendon, *Empire of Honor*, 34.

75   Ibid., 34; also 1 Corinthians.

## Chapter 4: Relationships Renewed

76 Joel Green, "The Gospel of Luke" in the *New International Commentary on the New Testament*, ed. Gordon Fee (Grand Rapids, MI: Eerdmans, 1997), 330.

77 Lendon, *Empire of Honour*, 50.

78 See Luke 5:27-32.

79 In addition to the stories we presented in the text, Luke 8:1-3 discusses women who regularly followed Jesus. Other stories about women are in Luke 7:11-17, 13:10-17, 18:15, and 21:1-4.

80 See Chapter 1.

81 Andreas J. Köstenberger, *John: Exegetical Commentary on the New Testament* (Grand Rapids, MI: Baker Academic, 2004), 158.

82 See Luke 24:1-12.

## Chapter 5: The Promise Becomes a Reality

83 Dallas Willard, *The Divine Conspiracy: Rediscovering Our Hidden Life in Christ* (New York: HarperOne, 1997), 13.

84 Aaron J. Kuecker, *The Spirit and the 'Other': Social Identity, Ethnicity and Intergroup Reconciliation in Luke-Acts.* (London: T & T Clark, 2011), 119.

85 Ibid., 120. Kuecker notes that "in these last days" in Isaiah 2:2 marks the final exaltation of Zion that prompts the nations to stream toward Jerusalem.

86  Craig Keener, *Acts: An Exegetical Commentary* (Grand Rapids, MI: Baker Academic, 2012), 875; also Isaiah 2:2; Hosea 3:5; Micah 4:1; and Daniel 2:28.

87  Darrell L. Bock, "Acts" in *Baker Exegetical Commentary on the New Testament,* ed. Robert W. Yarbrough and Robert H. Stein (Grand Rapids, MI: Baker Academic, 2007), 112; Ben Witherington III, *The Acts of the Apostles* (Grand Rapids, MI: Eerdmans, 2009), 140-143; Keener, *Acts,* 916-919. Some authors explain the signs in Acts 2:19-20 of the Joel quote as pointing to the signs of the resurrection. See F. F. Bruce, "The Book of Acts" in *The New International Commentary on the New Testament,* ed. Gordon Fee (Grand Rapids, MI: Eerdmans, 1988), 62.

88  Keener, *Acts,* 879.

89  Even within the most egalitarian and nonstructured societies, there still is basic division based on age and gender.

90  Keener, *Acts,* 882. He argues that Joel's prophecy also challenges class barriers, citing the reference to slaves.

91  Matthias Wenk, *Community Forming Power: The Socio-Ethical Role of the Spirit in Luke-Acts* (London: T & T Clark, 2004), 236.

92  Gerhard Lohfink, *Jesus and Community* (Philadelphia: Fortress Press, 1982), 93.

93  Kuecker, *The Spirit and the 'Other,'* 121.

94  Ibid., 121.

95  Victor Turner, *Dramas, Fields, and Metaphors: Symbolic Action in Human Society* (Ithaca, NY: Cornell University Press, 1974), 34.

96  Ibid., 34.

97  Ibid., 106.

98  Ibid., 112.

99  Victor Turner, *The Ritual Process: Structure and Anti-Structure* (Ithaca, NY: Cornell University Press, 1969), 134.

100 Ibid., 177.

101 Ibid., 93.

102 Christian Strecker, *Die liminale Theologie des Paulus* (Göttingen: Vandenhoeck & Ruprecht, 1999), 222; J. Paul Sampley, *Walking Between the Times* (Minneapolis: Fortress Press, 1991), 247; Gordon Fee, *Paul, the Spirit, and the People of God* (Peabody: Hendrickson Publishers, 1996), 51; also 1 Corinthians 5:17.

103 Karl Paul Donfried, *Paul, Thessalonica, and Early Christianity* (Grand Rapids, MI: Eerdmans, 2002), 234.

104 Sang Meyng Lee, *The Cosmic Drama of Salvation*, Wissenshaftliche Untersuchungen zum Neuen Testament, ed. Jörg Frey (Tübingen: Mohr Siebeck, 2010), 30.

105 C. Marvin Pate, *The End of the Age Has Come* (Grand Rapids, MI: Zondervan Publishing House, 1995), 153; Constantine R. Campbell, *Paul and Union with Christ* (Grand Rapids, MI: Zondervan, 2012), 408.

106 Robert Tannehill, *Dying and Rising with Christ* (Berlin: Verlag Alfred Töpelmann, 1996), 79.

107 Walter Bo Russell, *The Flesh/Spirit Conflict in Galatians* (New York: University Press of America, 1997), 2.

108 Galatians 5:16-17.

109 George Eldon Ladd, *A Theology of the New Testament* (Grand Rapids, MI: Eerdmans, 1974), 528.

110 2 Corinthians 4:14.

111 2 Corinthians 4:17.

112 Philippians 3:20-21.

113 Romans 4:13, 3:21-31 and Galatians 2:15-21.

114 Romans 1:16.

115 Romans 8:9.

116 1 Corinthians 12:13.

117 Michael J. Gorman, *Cruciformity: Paul's Narrative Spirituality of the Cross* (Grand Rapids, MI: Eerdmans, 2001), 352; also Galatians 3:28; 1 Corinthians 12:13; Colossians 3:11.

### *Chapter 6: Siblings in Christ*

118 What is informative with the use of sibling terminology is that in a patrilineal society (a type of society where name is traced through the father's side) relationships of mother and sister are the liminal relationships to the structural obligations of the patriline. This is because when a sister marries, her children belong to her husband's lineage. Therefore, interactions in those relationships are ones of affection and choice rather than obligation.

119 Joseph Hellerman, *The Ancient Church as Family* (Sheffield: Sheffield Phoenix Press, 2007), 92.

120 Ibid., 92.

121 Lohfink, *Jesus and Community*, 108.

122 S. Scott Bartchy, *Call No Man Father* (Grand Rapids, MI: Baker Academic Forthcoming), 37. There are various viewpoints on whether the use of sibling terminology reflects or undermines patriarchal household structure. Bartchy, Lohfink, and Hellerman argue that sibling relationships undermined patriarchy. Karl Olav Sandnes ("Equality within Patriarchal Structures" in *Constructing Early Christian Families: Family as Social Reality and Metaphor.* ed Halvor Moxnes, London: Routledge, 1997, 150-166.) sees egalitarian structures as emerging in patriarchy. Reider Aasgaard (*My Beloved Brothers and Sisters! Christian Siblingship in Paul* Peabody, MA: T & T Clark International, 2004) argues for a metaphorical use which shaped relationships.

123 Robert L.Brawley, "From Reflex to Reflections? Identity in Philippians 2:6-11 and Its Context" in *Reading Paul in Context: Explorations in Identity Formation*, ed. Kathy Ehrensperger and J. Brian Tucker (London: T & T Clark, 2010), 134.

124 Aasgaard, *My Beloved Brothers and Sisters!*, 312.

125 Hellerman, *The Ancient Church as Family*, 113.

126 David A. deSilva, *Honor, Patronage, Kinship & Purity* (Downers Grove, IL: InterVarsity Press, 2010), 169.

127 Hellerman, *The Ancient Church as Family*, 113.

128 Trevor J. Burke, *Family Matters: A Socio-Historical Study of Kinship Metaphors in 1 Thessalonians*, Vol. 247, JSNT, ed. Stanley E. Porter (Peabody, MA: T & T Clark International, 2003), 167.

129 Lohfink, *Jesus and Community*, 100.

130 Volker Rabens, *The Holy Spirit and Ethics in Paul*, Wissenshaftliche Untersuchungen zum Neuen Testament 2, Reihe, ed. by Jörg Frey (Tübingen: Mohr Siebeck, 2010), 136.

131 Rabens, *The Holy Spirit and Ethics in Paul*, 238.

132 Lohfink, *Jesus and Community*, 99.

133 Ben C. Dunson, *Individual and Community in Paul's Letter to the Romans*, Wissenschaftliche Untersuchungen zum Neuen Testament 2, Reihe, ed. Jörg Frey (Tübingen: Mohr Siebeck, 2012), 129.

134 Gerd Theissen, *The Religion of the Earliest Churches* (Minneapolis: Fortress Press, 1999), 72.

135 Erik M. Heen, "Phil 2:6-11 and Resistance to Local Timocratic Rule: Isa Theo and the Cult of the Emperor in the East" in *Paul and the Roman Imperial Order*, ed. Richard A. Hosley (Harrisburg, PA: Trinty Press International, 2004), 129.

136 Heen, "Phil 2:6-11," 150; also Ephesians 5:21.

137 1 Corinthians 11:22.

138 Romans 14:10; 1 Corinthians 3:21; Galatians 5:26; and Philippians 2:3.

139 Galatians 5:26; Colossians 3:8; 1 Corinthians 3:18; and 1 Peter 2:1.

140 deSilva, *Honor, Patronage, Kinship & Purity*, 77.

141 Romans 12:16 and Ephesians 4:2.

142 Philippians 2:3 and Romans 2:8.

143 deSilva, *Honor, Patronage, Kinship & Purity*, 77.

144 Gorman, *Cruciformity*, 233.

145 Joseph Hellerman, *Reconstructing Honor in Roman Philippi* (Cambridge: Cambridge University Press, 2005), 165.

146 Romans 5:5; Galatians 4:6-7; Philippians 1:8; and John 13:34-35.

147 Ben Witherington, *Conflict and Community in Corinth: A Socio-Rhetorical Commentary on 1 and 2 Corinthians* (Grand Rapids, MI: Eerdmans, 1995), 269; also Romans 5:6-8.

148 Gordon D. Fee, *God's Empowering Presence: The Holy Spirit in the Letters of Paul.* (Peabody, MA: Hendrickson, 1994), 201.

149 1 Thessalonians 2:14.

150 Ephesians 5:2.

151 Michelle Lee, *Paul, the Stoics, and the Body of Christ*, Society for New Testament Studies, Vol. 137, ed. Lee Court (Cambridge: Cambridge University Press, 2006), 184.

152 Robert Banks, *Paul's Idea of Community* (Peabody, MA: Hendrickson Publishers, 1994), 54.

153 Fee, *God's Empowering Presence*, 201.

154 Lee, *Paul, the Stoics, and the Body of Christ,* 183.

155 1 Corinthians 12-14.

156 Ephesians 4:2 and Galatians 5:16-26.

157 Roy E. Ciampa and Brian S. Rosner, *The First Letter to the Corinthians* (Grand Rapids, MI: Eerdmans, 2010), 640.

158 2 Corinthians 9:2.

159 Galatians 6:10.

160 John 13:35.

## *Chapter 7: Siblings in the World*

161 S. Scott Bartchy, *First-Century Slavery & the Interpretation of 1 Corinthians 7:21* (Eugene, OR: Wipf and Stock Publishers, 2003), 153.

162 Bruce Hansen, *All of You Are One*, (London: T & T Clark, 2010), 84.

163 Kathy Ehrensperger, *Paul and the Dynamics of Power*, ed. Mark Goodacre (New York: T & T Clark, 2007), 192.

164 Ehrensperger, *Paul and the Dynamics of Power*, 192.

165 Hansen, *All of You Are One*, 166.

166 J. Brian Tucker, "Baths, Baptism, and Patronage: The Continuing Role of Roman Social Identity in Corinth" in *Reading Paul in Context: Explorations in Identity Formation*, ed. Kathy Ehrensperger and J. Brian Tucker (London: T & T Clark, 2010), 177.

167 Bartchy, *First-Century Slavery*, 151.

168 Ibid., 151.

169 1 Corinthians 7:7-24.

170 Bartchy, *First-Century Slavery*, 151.

171 Ehrensperger, *Paul and the Dynamics of Power*, 195.

172 Philemon 1:14.

173 Philemon 1:16.

174  Pauline Hogan, *No Longer Male and Female: Interpreting Galatians 3:28 in Early Christianity* (London: T & T Clark, 2008), 32; Philemon 1:17.

175  Hogan, *No Longer Male and Female,* 32.

176  An overview of the scholarly discussion can be found in Ronald W. Pierce, "Contemporary Evangelicals for Gender Equality" in *Discovering Biblical Equality,* eds. Ronald W. Pierce and Rebecca Merrill Groothuis (Downers Grove, IL: InterVarsity Press Academic, 2005), 58-78.

177  Hansen, *All of You Are One,* 135.

178  1 Corinthians 7:1-7.

169  Hogan, *No Longer Male and Female,* 38; ,175.

180  Hogan, *No Longer Male and Female,* 32; Alan G. Paget, *As Christ Submits to the Church: A Biblical Understanding of Leadership and Mutual Submission* (Grand Rapids, MI: Baker Academics, 2011), 69.

181  1 Corinthians 7:12-16.

182  Roy E. Ciampa and Brian S. Rosner, *The First Letter to the Corinthians* (Grand Rapids, MI: Eerdmans, 2010), 296.

183  1 Corinthians 7:25-35.

184  Hansen, *All of You Are One,* 138.

185  Gilbert Bilezikian, *Beyond Sex Roles* (Grand Rapids, MI: Baker Books, 2006), 134.

186  Ephesians 5:22-6:9.

187 Peter T. O'Brian, *The Letter to the Ephesians* (Grand Rapids, MI: Eerdmans, 1999), 409-438, argues that Paul is reinforcing the natural order of subordination of wife, children, and slave. Some form of this argument is used by those who argue that Paul or the writer of Ephesians is reverting back to more conservative views of gender relationships within the household. See also Harold W. Hoehner, *Ephesians: An Exegetical Commentary* (Grand Rapids, MI: Baker Academic Books, 2002), 720-784; Clinton Arnold, *Ephesians: Exegetical Commentary on the New Testament* (Grand Rapids, MI: Zondervan, 2010), 363-410.

188 Craig S. Keener, *Paul, Women, and Wives: Marriage and Women's Ministry in the Letters of Paul* (Grand Rapids, MI: Baker Academic, 1993), 185. See also Ephesians 5:21-33.

189 Gordon D. Fee, "Hermeneutics and the Gender Debate," in *Discovering Biblical Equality*, eds. Ronald W. Pierce and Rebecca Merrill Groothuis (Downers Grove, IL: InterVarsity Press Academic, 2005), 364-381.

190 Ibid., 379.

### *Chapter 8: The Prickly Passage*

191 Keener, *Paul, Women, and Wives,* 101.

192 Harold W. Hoehner, *Ephesians: An Exegetical Commentary* (Grand Rapids, MI: Baker Academic Books, 2002), 87.

193 Aida Besancon Spencer, *1 Timothy: A New Covenant Commentary* (Eugene, OR: Cascade Books, 2013), 14.

194 Clinton Arnold, *Ephesians: Exegetical Commentary on the New Testament* (Grand Rapids, MI: Zondervan, 2010), 30.

195 Ibid., 30.

196 Ibid., 31.

197 Spencer, *1 Timothy,* 16.

198 Arnold, *Ephesians,* 33.

199 Ibid., 30.

200 Spencer, *1 Timothy,* 15.

201 Keener, Craig, *Acts: An Exegetical Commentary: 15:1-23:35,* Vol. 3 (Grand Rapids, MI: Baker Academic, 2014), 2876.

202 Keener, 2887.

203 Spencer, *1 Timothy,* 16.

204 Gary G. Hoag, *Wealth in Ancient Ephesus and the First Letter to Timothy: Fresh Insights from Ephesiaca by Xenophon of Ephesus* (Winona Lake, IN: Eisenbrauns, 2015), 42.

205 Ibid., 35.

206 Ibid., 40.

207 Ibid., 32.

208 Ibid., 51.

209 Ibid., 50.

210 Ibid., 51.

211 Ibid., 51.

212 Keener, *Acts*, 2827.

213 Ibid., 2830.

214 Acts 19:26.

215 Spencer, *1 Timothy*, 18; McKnight, *Kingdom Conspiracy*, 10.

216 Philip R. Towner, *The Letters to Timothy and Titus* (Grand Rapids, MI: Eerdmans, 2006), 41.

217 Spencer, *1 Timothy*, 18-19.

218 Fredrick J. Long, 2015, "A Wife in Relation to a Husband: Greek Discourse Pragmatic and Cultural Evidence for Interpreting 1 Timothy 2:11-15," The Journal of Inductive Biblical Studies, Vol. 2: Issue 2, 18.

219 Ibid., 19.

220 Ibid., 23.

221 Ibid., 27.

222 Ibid., 31. For a fuller description of the new Roman woman, see Bruce Winter, *Roman Wives, Roman Widows: The Appearance of New Women and the Pauline Communities* (Grand Rapids, MI: Eerdmans, 2003).

223 Hoag, *Wealth in Ancient Ephesus*, 65.

224 Ibid., 65.

225 Ibid., 65.

226 Ibid., 70.

227 Long, "A Wife in Relation to a Husband," 27.

228 Philip B. Payne, *Man and Woman, One in Christ: An Exegetical and Theological Study of Paul's Letters* (Grand Rapids, MI: Zondervan, 2009), 319.

229 NIV.

230 See Cynthia Westfall, *Paul and Gender: Reclaiming the Apostle's Vision for Men and Women in Christ* (Grand Rapids, MI: Baker Academic, 2016) and Long, "A Wife in Relation to a Husband."

231 Long, "A Wife in Relation to a Husband," 14.

232 Ibid., 36.

233 Ibid., 32.

234 Payne, *Man and Woman*, 314.

235 Ibid., 320.

236 For a full discussion, see Payne, *Man and Woman*, 337-359.

237 Ibid., 327.

238 Westfall, *Paul and Gender,* 292.

239 Ibid., 291.

240 Long, "A Wife in Relation to a Husband," 36.

241 Payne and others give an alternative interpretation citing that Paul was referring to women in general. He suggests that women were self-asserting authority and teaching heresy, presumably from the Artemis cult. Thus, the emphasis on learning, they were to learn before they taught.

242 Long, "A Wife in Relation to a Husband," 41.

243 Hoag, *Wealth in Ancient Ephesus,* 99.

244 Long, "A Wife in Relation to a Husband," 37.

245 Payne infers that the situation was women teaching false doctrine and that women were to learn, which is the opposite of being deceived. Paul was asking women not to teach because they had not learned appropriately and were still teaching false doctrine from their background with Artemis, just as Eve did not have appropriate knowledge of what God said and was also deceived. Payne, *Man and Woman,* 351.

246 Payne, *Man and Woman,* 351.

247 Hoag, *Wealth in Ancient Ephesus,* 92.

248 1 Timothy 5:1a.

## *Chapter 9: Conclusion*

249 Ken Wytsma, *The Myth of Inequality: Uncovering the Roots of Injustice and Privilege* (Downers Grove, IL: IVP Books, 2007).

250 Micah 6:8.

251 Sue Edwards, Kelly Mathews, and Henry J. Rogers, *Mixed Ministry: Working Together as Brothers and Sisters in an Oversexed Society* (Grand Rapids, MI: Kregel, 2008).

# Biographies of the Authors

Dr. A. Sue Russell is Professor of Missions and Contextual Studies at Asbury Theological Seminary. She has an MDiv and ThM From Talbot Theological Seminary as well as three doctorates: a DMiss from Biola University, a PhD in Linguistic Anthropology from La Trobe University, and a PhD in Early Christian History from UCLA. She has spent 20 years mentoring, empowering, and encouraging graduate and undergraduate men and women to live and work together as brothers and sisters in Christ. She spent 15 years in S.E. Asia working with and learning from Galat* brothers and sisters, translating the entire Bible into their language. She is the current president of the Association of Professors of Mission (APM) and is a frequent presenter at academic conferences. She has authored numerous articles and two books.

Dr. Jackie Roese is the Founder and President of The Marcella Project, a ministry committed to "ennobling" women through Scripture – focused on teaching, training and dialogue. She has a MA in Christian Education from Dallas Theological Seminary and a D.Min. in Preaching from Gordon-Conwell Theological Seminary. Jackie spent eight years serving in a mega-church as Teaching Pastor to Women as well as serving on the Sunday morning preaching team. She has taught women's Bible studies for over 20 years. She has written more than 15 Bible studies and authored three books.

*A pseudonym.

Printed in Great Britain
by Amazon